Endorse

Who among us does not want more out of life? We try all sorts of things, but many times all we need do is look inwardly to effect the kind of change that we want in our lives. You can *be* more and *do* more if you know where your help comes from. When you know that you are not in this race by yourself, it changes the entire game and opens up a whole new world of opportunities and possibilities. Are you ready for change in your life? If so, then you are ready for Pastor André's approach to winning and achieving victory in your life.

—Tim Timberlake, co-pastor,
Christian Faith Center, Creedmoor, North Carolina

In a world full of uncertainty, disappointments, and frustrations, it's easy to see why most people tolerate failure. Through this book, not only does Pastor André inspire you to win, but he also equips you with the spiritual tools you need to triumph in every area of life. André Butler is a personal friend whom I greatly respect. He's also a proven leader with wisdom beyond his years, qualified by God to help you fulfill your divine destiny.

—Dr. John Barton, president,
John Barton Ministries and author of *Awaken Your Dream*

I am so excited to be able to recommend Pastor Andre Butler's new book *You Can Win*. I've known Pastor Andre for many years and he truly is a man of God, full of integrity and faith. He is anointed by God to teach His Word and you will be uplifted as he shares with you how to win no matter what problem you may be facing.

Rev. Kate McVeigh
Evangelist/Author/Radio/TV Personality
www.katemcveigh.org

YOU CAN
WIN

YOU CAN
WIN

slaying the goliaths in your life

André Butler

foreword by MiChelle Butler

HIGHERLIFE

DEVELOPMENT SERVICES, INC

Oviedo, Florida

You Can Win by André Butler

Published by HigherLife Development Services, Inc.
400 Fontana Circle
Building 1—Suite 105
Oviedo, Florida 32765
(407) 563-4806
www.ahigherlife.com

Unless otherwise noted, Scriptures are taken from the King James Version of the Bible.

Scriptures marked AMP are taken from the Amplified® Bible, Copyright © 1954, 1958, 1962, 1964, 1965, 1987 by The Lockman Foundation. Used by permission. (www.lockman.org)

Scriptures marked MSG are from The Message. Copyright © 1993. Used by permission of NavPress Publishing Group.

Scriptures marked NLT are from The New Living Translation: Holy Bible. New Living Translation copyright© 1996, 2004, 2007 by Tyndale House Foundation. Used by permission of Tyndale House Publishers Inc., Carol Stream, Illinois 60188. All rights reserved.

ISBN: 978-1-935245-93-3
12 13 14 15 16 17 — 9 8 7 6 5 4 3 2 1
Printed in the United States of America

Dedication

To my Tiffany Diamond and my three little princesses: Alexis, Angie, and April.

I love you all more than I can express.

Acknowledgments

I WOULD LIKE TO GIVE honor to my Lord and Savior, Jesus Christ, who has saved me and given me the honor of helping Him save the world. Also to my parents and sisters, Bishop Keith Butler, Pastor Deborah Butler, Pastor MiChelle Butler, and Minister Kristina Butler. Without all of you, I would not be who I am. I also would like to acknowledge Rev. Kenneth E. Hagin, Rev. Kenneth W. Hagin, Kenneth and Gloria Copeland, and the many other outstanding men and women of God who have taught me the word of faith. I am forever grateful!

A 28-Day Challenge

STEP 3: FOLLOW THE PLAN

STEP 4: DO YOUR VICTORY DANCE

Foreword

HAVING A FRONT-ROW SEAT to my big brother's life—the good, the bad, and the ugly—I can say that if anyone is qualified to write on the subject of winning, it is my brother, André. I have had the privilege of watching him live his life honoring God and walking in integrity, not just in the pulpit and in ministry, but also in everyday life. He handled all the struggles and challenges we faced being PKs as children and teenagers and then following in our father's footsteps.

You Can Win is a practical manual of what André has walked out in his own life. It is not surprising to me that God is using my brother to deliver such a powerful revelation to this generation that we cannot be defeated and we will not quit. In a time when godlessness seems to be the order of the day, *You Can Win* provides sound, Scripture-based solutions to so many challenges that people face today. André offers solutions that apply to whatever circumstance you may be struggling with right now. He includes practical step-by-step illustrations from God's Word that will help you get back on the victory road.

In my fifteen-plus years of being in the ministry, one of the greatest epidemics I've seen among people is a lack of identity of who they are in Christ, which is why I was honored to write the foreword for this book. People are searching in all the wrong places for the victory that God has already provided for them on the cross. André does a great job reminding you who you are and how to grab hold of your victory. I particularly love how he teaches you to go through a difficult situation—not just park there—and how to look up and apply God's solution so that you can go on to do your victory dance.

So get yourself up, get your game face on, put on your victory shoes, and prepare to get your victory dance on! You can win!

—Pastor MiChelle Butler,
MiChelle Butler Ministries
Southfield, Michigan

STEP 1:

LOOK UP

You Can Win

In all these things we are more than conquerors through him that loved us.

—ROMANS 8:37

IT'S DAY ONE OF our twenty-eight-day challenge. You may not even know what that involves yet, but I want to give you a gift: hope. You may be facing some very dire situations. Your bank account may be running on empty. Your spouse may not be exactly what you dreamed of at the altar. Your children may be acting crazy (or driving you crazy). Your body may be telling you it's falling apart. So I want you to begin with hope. In the next twenty-eight days, you'll see that God has victory for you in all these areas. We'll be reading dozens of Scripture verses that prove this. The world around you has no assurance of victory, but I have some exciting news for you: If you're a follower of Jesus, whatever you're facing in life, you can win. This book gives a plan based on God's Word that will help you experience victory in your life, no matter what situation you face. You'll learn the four steps to that victory and how to live them out—not just while you're reading this book but long after you reach the last page.

1. Look up. You'll learn how to take your eyes off your problems (where the Enemy wants you focused) and instead focus on the Lord. One brings problems and the other brings solutions.

2. Go through. You'll learn that when challenges come along, you can spend time in the valley of the shadow of death or you can learn how to go through it. You can do that quickly or slowly, and you'll learn the road signs to look for.

3. Follow the plan. You'll study specific areas of life where you may need victory, and you'll learn God's prescribed solutions to bring you that victory. These areas include your marriage (or lack thereof), your spouse, your children, your finances, your health, addictions, and more.

4. Do your victory dance. By the time you reach day twenty-eight, I know you'll be full of faith, but I want to help you to act on your faith by getting you to praise God for the victory—before you see it.

How the Challenge Works

Here's how the twenty-eight day challenge works:

☐ **Step one:** Get the book.
☐ **Step two:** Keep up with the readings every day.
☐ **Step three:** Meet weekly with a small group to discuss what
 you're learning and the questions at the end of each section.
☐ **Step four:** Give a book to a friend and encourage him or her
 to take the twenty-eight-day challenge also.

It's very helpful to do this twenty-eight-day challenge with other believers. If you don't have a faith group or small group, then find a group of likeminded believers who want to pursue all that God has for them. They'll provide the support, encouragement, and sometimes correction that you need. Don't worry; you'll do the same for them.

If You're Going to Win . . .

If you've read any of my other books or hung around me for more than a few minutes, you know that I firmly believe God's desire is to prosper you. That's not my opinion, of course; the Bible is extremely clear on that. If we're not careful, however, we can start thinking that a prosperous life is a life where we never face any difficulty. That is just not biblical. The prosperous life is a victorious life. It's a life where you prosper because you overcome the Enemy. That doesn't mean you don't face battles—but it does mean you are victorious in them. "Many are the afflictions of the righteous, but the LORD delivereth him out of them all" (Psalm 34:19). "The just come shall come out of trouble" (Proverbs 12:13).

Since this book is about winning, you need to know exactly what you want to win and exactly where you need victory. Spend some time thinking about areas in your life where you need a checkmark in the "win" column. Some of those areas will be very obvious—a broken marriage, a rebellious child, a body in need of healing. Other areas may be hidden—such as dreams you've had for decades, dreams that are so dormant it's painful to even think about resurrecting them. List them on the "victory pages" that follow. As you go through the next twenty-eight days, you'll be adding to your victory pages, but I'd like you start right now by simply filling in the first two points on each page: areas where you need victory and a few words about the current situation.

Spend some time thinking about areas in your life where you need a checkmark in the "win" column.

You'll update your victory pages throughout the next twenty-eight days, particularly as you come to the end of each step. By the time you complete the challenge, I know you will begin to see victories and breakthroughs.

Don't wait until you get into the end zone to start dancing, however. Start dancing now because your victory is on the way!

Victory Is Coming!

1. Area where I need victory:

_____

_____

2. Current situation and today's date:

_____

_____

3. Scripture promises regarding this area:

_____

_____

_____

_____

4. What God is showing me that I need to be doing so I can experience victory in this area:

_____

_____

_____

_____

(continued on next page)

_____

_____

_____

_____

_____

5. What God is showing me that I need to stop doing so I can experience victory in this area:

_____

_____

_____

_____

_____

_____

_____

6. Victory!

_____

_____

_____

_____

_____

Victory Is Coming!

Fill in #1 and #2 today.

1. Area where I need victory:

_____

_____

2. Current situation and today's date:

_____

_____

Leave the rest blank; you'll fill these in during the next twenty-eight days.

3. Scripture promises regarding this area:

_____

_____

_____

_____

4. What God is showing me that I need to be doing so I can experience victory in this area:

_____

_____

_____

_____

(continued on next page)

_____

_____

_____

_____

_____

5. What God is showing me that I need to stop doing so I can experience victory in this area:

_____

_____

_____

_____

_____

_____

6. Victory!

_____

_____

_____

_____

_____

Victory Is Coming!

Fill in #1 and #2 today.

1. Area where I need victory:

_____

_____

2. Current situation and today's date:

_____

_____

Leave the rest blank; you'll fill these in during the next twenty-eight days.

3. Scripture promises regarding this area:

_____

_____

_____

_____

4. What God is showing me that I need to be doing so I can experience victory in this area:

_____

_____

_____

_____

(continued on next page)

_____

_____

_____

_____

_____

5. What God is showing me that I need to stop doing so I can experience victory in this area:

_____

_____

_____

_____

_____

_____

6. Victory!

_____

_____

_____

_____

_____

Victory Is Coming!

Fill in #1 and #2 today.

1. Area where I need victory:

_____

_____

2. Current situation and today's date:

_____

_____

Leave the rest blank; you'll fill these in during the next twenty-eight days.

3. Scripture promises regarding this area:

_____

_____

_____

_____

4. What God is showing me that I need to be doing so I can experience victory in this area:

_____

_____

_____

_____

(continued on next page)

_____

_____

_____

_____

_____

5. What God is showing me that I need to stop doing so I can experience victory in this area:

_____

_____

_____

_____

_____

_____

6. Victory!

_____

_____

_____

_____

_____

Victory Is Coming!

Fill in #1 and #2 today.

1. Area where I need victory:

_____

_____

2. Current situation and today's date:

_____

_____

Leave the rest blank; you'll fill these in during the next twenty-eight days.

3. Scripture promises regarding this area:

_____

_____

_____

_____

4. What God is showing me that I need to be doing so I can experience victory in this area:

_____

_____

_____

_____

(continued on next page)

_____

_____

_____

_____

5. What God is showing me that I need to stop doing so I can experience victory in this area:

_____

_____

_____

_____

_____

6. Victory!

_____

_____

_____

_____

Victory Is Coming!

Fill in #1 and #2 today.

1. Area where I need victory:

_____

_____

2. Current situation and today's date:

_____

_____

Leave the rest blank; you'll fill these in during the next twenty-eight days.

3. Scripture promises regarding this area:

_____

_____

_____

_____

4. What God is showing me that I need to be doing so I can experience victory in this area:

_____

_____

_____

_____

(continued on next page)

_____

_____

_____

_____

5. What God is showing me that I need to stop doing so I can experience victory in this area:

_____

_____

_____

_____

_____

6. Victory!

_____

_____

_____

_____

Victory Is Coming!

Fill in #1 and #2 today.

1. Area where I need victory:

_____

_____

2. Current situation and today's date:

_____

_____

Leave the rest blank; you'll fill these in during the next twenty-eight days.

3. Scripture promises regarding this area:

_____

_____

_____

_____

4. What God is showing me that I need to be doing so I can experience victory in this area:

_____

_____

_____

_____

(continued on next page)

_____

_____

_____

_____

_____

5. What God is showing me that I need to stop doing so I can experience victory in this area:

_____

_____

_____

_____

_____

_____

6. Victory!

_____

_____

_____

_____

_____

Victory Is Coming!

Fill in #1 and #2 today.

1. Area where I need victory:

_____

_____

2. Current situation and today's date:

_____

_____

Leave the rest blank; you'll fill these in during the next twenty-eight days.

3. Scripture promises regarding this area:

_____

_____

_____

_____

4. What God is showing me that I need to be doing so I can experience victory in this area:

_____

_____

_____

_____

(continued on next page)

_____

_____

_____

_____

_____

5. What God is showing me that I need to stop doing so I can experience victory in this area:

_____

_____

_____

_____

_____

_____

_____

6. Victory!

_____

_____

_____

_____

_____

Victory Is Coming!

1. Area where I need victory:

_____

_____

2. Current situation and today's date:

_____

_____

3. Scripture promises regarding this area:

_____

_____

_____

_____

4. What God is showing me that I need to be doing so I can experience victory in this area:

_____

_____

_____

_____

(continued on next page)

_____

_____

_____

_____

_____

5. What God is showing me that I need to stop doing so I can experience victory in this area:

_____

_____

_____

_____

_____

_____

6. Victory!

_____

_____

_____

_____

Day 2

You Are an Overcomer

Who is he that overcometh the world, but he that believeth that Jesus is the Son of God?

—1 John 5:5

Y OU CAN WIN. THAT'S what this entire book is about, summed up in three short words. How I'm going to get you to believe that will take a few more words. By the time you reach day twenty-eight in this challenge, I want you to fully believe that you can overcome any circumstance, any difficulty, any giant, any mountain, any bad habit, and any persecution that's in your life. You *can* win—but don't take my word for it. Here's what the Word of God says:

> Whosoever believeth that Jesus is the Christ is born of God: and every one that loveth him that begat loveth him also that is begotten of him. By this we know that we love the children of God, when we love God, and keep his commandments. For this is the love of God, that we keep his commandments: and his commandments are not grievous. For whatsoever is born of God overcometh the world: and this is the victory that overcometh the world, even our faith.
>
> Who is he that overcometh the world, but he that believeth that Jesus is the Son of God?
>
> —1 John 5:1–5

When the Bible says you are "born of God," that is not a phrase to take lightly. In fact, the phrases "of God" and "born of God" appear over and over again in chapters 4 and 5 of the book of 1 John because there is something very significant about being born of God. You become a new class of being. You go from lightweight to heavyweight. You go from being a son of man to being a son of God. Another way of saying it, of course, is being "born again." So if you are born again, you are born of God and the rest of this verse is for you. (If you are not born again, this would be a good time to make that decision. You don't want to miss out on the next twenty-eight days…or the rest of your life.)

These verses don't say, "Whoever is born of God *can* overcome" or *"will* overcome." They say if you are born of God, you overcome. You *are* an overcomer. You have already been overcoming the world. Overcoming the world is what you do. You are not a loser; you are a winner. You are more than a conqueror through Him who loves you, through the One who always causes you to triumph (Romans 8:37). If you are born of God, then being an overcomer is your nature. That is what you do.

In fact, you have been overcoming the world for a while now. When you made Jesus the Lord of your life, you overcame all the power of the Enemy that had been working in your life to keep you from that moment. You over-came it when you decided to receive Him as Lord of your life. You overcame sin to get to that point—and to get to this very moment where you're reading the words on this page. The fact that you're reading this means you overcame your flesh today because there are many people who did not. They are still on the pillow or they are

You *are* an overcomer. You don't have to try to become one; you already are one.

out at the bars or watching TV. They did not overcome their flesh, but you overcame your flesh and are taking the twenty-eight day challenge, showing the Devil once again that he doesn't run your life. You run your life. God runs your life.

If you think about it, you could list dozens of situations in your past where you've had to believe God—money problems, sickness in your body, issues with your kids or your spouse or your boss. These are all obstacles you had to overcome, and you did overcome them because you learned how to get hold of the Word of God. You overcame all those problems and gained the peace that passes understanding. So you *are* an overcomer. You don't have to try to become one; you already are one.

Three Areas to Overcome

When we talk about winning and being overcomers, there are three main areas where we overcome the world.

1. Sin. "For this is the love of God, that we keep his commandments: and his commandments are not grievous" (1 John 5:3). His commandments aren't grievous or tough to keep—at least not for those who are born of God. They are tough to keep for those who are not sons of God, but if you are born again, you have access to Jesus. He said, "My yoke is easy, and my burden [what I require you to carry] is light" (Matthew 11:30).

A few years ago, when Tiffany and I were moving, some men from the church helped out on moving day. Among my workout equipment were some barbells. The weight of them was challenging for me, but one of the men helping us picked them up like they weighed nothing. He was huge, with arms as big as my legs, so for him those barbells were nothing.

God wants you to know that when it comes to sin, if you're a son of God, then you've got muscles that the Devil doesn't want anything to do with. For you to overcome that silly temptation that the Devil sends your way is nothing because you are an overcomer. That is what you do. Sons of God consistently overcome the temptation to sin.

2. Tribulation and trouble. "In the world ye shall have tribulation: but be of good cheer; I have overcome the world" (John 16:33). Satan will send pressure your way. He will try to attack your family, your body, your career, your peace of mind, and any other area of your life that he can. The good news is that you always triumph: "In all these things we are more than conquerors through him that loved us" (Romans 8:37). That is what you do. Sons of God consistently overcome tribulation and trouble.

3. Satan. Revelation 12:11 tells us that you overcome the Devil by the blood of the Lamb and the word of your testimony. How do you do this? "And this is the victory . . . even our faith" (1 John 5:4). Faith is total persuasion, total reliance, and 100-percent confidence in God and in His Word. Faith is not of the mind. It's of the heart. It exists despite negative circumstances. The Bible says, "We walk by faith, not by sight" (2 Corinthians 5:7). So if it is sight, it is not faith. And if it is faith, it is not sight. That is what you do. Sons of God consistently walk by faith, not by sight, and they consistently overcome Satan.

In 2007, the New England Patriots had an 18–0 record leading up to the Super Bowl—and were one of only a handful of teams to have ever done that. They had one play that was their means of success. Quarterback Tom Brady would drop back. He would look for receiver Randy Moss, who was running about forty yards down the field. Brady would throw it, and Moss would catch it and head into the end zone for a touchdown. If the game was close and they thought they were going to lose, they would just run that play and it would be all over. That was their means of success. Of course, they lost the Super Bowl, but that's another story.

You, too, have a never-fail touchdown pass—that thing that is going to bring you out of whatever you're dealing with. It is your faith. That's why it is so important for you to maintain your faith. Faith is what will see you through. Whatever obstacle you face as you're reading these words—whatever your mountain, your giant, or your Red Sea—you can overcome it by using your faith. If you don't believe me, just read Hebrews 11. We call it the Faith Hall of Fame, and I think it's still being written. (If so, I want my name in it.) The way you get in this Hall of Fame is by walking by faith. Just read about what those heroes of the faith went through, and it will encourage your faith.

I don't know what your situation is, but I do know that the same God who performed all those miracles for everyone listed in Hebrews 11 will do the same for you. Whatever you are dealing with, you can overcome it by using your faith. Start agreeing with the Holy Ghost and say, "I am an overcomer. I can win, and I will win in Jesus' name."

Stop Being Afraid of Your Problems

"I have overcome the world."

—John 16:33

You may have started day three feeling a little heavy because you were thinking about all the situations you're dealing with, but I have good news for you: "These things I have spoken unto you, that in me ye might have peace. In the world ye shall have tribulation: but be of good cheer; I have overcome the world" (John 16:33). The kind of peace Jesus is talking about here is not peace from an absence of war. It is actually a peace that guards your heart and your mind in the midst of war. It is peace in the midst of trials. It is a peace that passes understanding. That's what God says you can have.

In fact, these words from John 16:33 are almost the last words Jesus shared with His disciples before His crucifixion, so we have to believe He chose them well. He knew what was coming for them, and He gave these words as a warning that things might not always be smooth sailing. But they were also given as a promise that if they focused on Him, He would give them peace in the midst of the storms. Why? Because He has overcome the world.

And these words are for you, too, no matter what you face here on the third day of our twenty-eight-day challenge.

A number of years ago, I was going through a difficult situation. The Lord finally said to me, "Why don't you do what you know you're supposed to do?" I knew He was referring to Philippians 4: "Be careful for nothing; but in every thing by prayer and supplication with thanksgiving let your requests be made known unto God. And the peace of God, which passeth all understanding, shall keep your hearts and minds through Christ Jesus" (vv. 6–7). He was telling me to stop focusing on my problem and instead focus on Him in prayer. So I did—and guess what happened? The situation got worse! But I had such peace that I almost forgot about it. I literally said, "Shouldn't I be worrying? Shouldn't I be flipping out by now?" I was shocked that I had such peace. What the Bible said was true.

If you are having a hard time doing that, then get in the Word and read what God said. Read it, confess it, and think on it. Make it your own so that you could preach it yourself if you had to. The Word will produce that peace so you can be joyful no matter what's going on. God doesn't want you going up and down emotionally based on your life's circumstances, because that is what the world does. Remember what we learned yesterday? You are a son or daughter of God. You have available to you the peace that passes understanding. You also have God on your side, and He has promised that He is going to bring you out victoriously.

I don't know about you, but there's one part of John 16:33 that is not one of my favorite prophecies in the Bible: "In the world ye shall have tribulation." That verse is true—and not just for Christians. It is true for non-Christians as well. The Bible, however, has a promise for those who follow Jesus: "Many are the afflictions of the righteous: but the LORD delivereth him out of them all" (Psalm 34:19). The unrighteous have afflictions, too, but they haven't decided to side with the Lord, so they don't get delivered from them all. But if you are following Jesus, He promises to deliver you from *all* your

God has a way of making your trouble work *for* you, not against you. Satan can't even win when he attacks you.

afflictions—because He has overcome the world. Because of that, you can "be of good cheer." That literally means "to take courage." In other words, don't shrink away. Go ahead and face that trouble. James 1:2 says, "Count it all joy when you fall into divers temptations." If you have been counting it as depression or sadness, you need a recount. You need to start counting your joy. James adds that when you go through tough times, that builds your patience. God has a way of making your trouble work *for* you, not against you. Satan can't even win when he attacks you.

If Jesus stated, "I have overcome the world," and you are His follower, then the only way Satan can hurt you is if you stop believing Jesus has overcome Satan—that is, if you lay down your faith. Satan is already defeated and disarmed, even though he doesn't act like it.

Think of it this way. Say you were in a store and some dude walks up, and it looks like he has a gun in his pocket. He's trying to hold you up by saying, "Give me your money!" One of your friends is around the corner, and they see that what he really has is a Snickers bar but it looks like a gun. At that moment, you've got a decision to make. You can either be held up by a Snickers bar or you can put an end to this thing.

That's all Satan has got. He's already defeated. You are in a game with a teammate who has already won the championship—Jesus. He already defeated Satan. He already overcame the world. He already paved the way for your success, and now He's walking with you arm-in-arm through the battle, making sure you are victorious, too.

> Who shall separate us from the love of Christ? shall tribulation, or distress, or persecution, or famine, or nakedness, or peril, or sword? As it is written, For thy sake we are killed all the day long; we are accounted as sheep for the slaughter. Nay, in all these things we are more than conquerors through him that loved us.
>
> —Romans 8:35–37

Whatever you are dealing with right now, you can say, "I am more than a conqueror through Him who loves me, through Him who overcame the world, through Him who dealt with tribulation, distress, persecution, lack, and danger." In all those things, Jesus overcame. Now He says to you, "You can do the same thing. I'm walking with you. Through Me you can overcome it all."

No wonder the Bible says, "I can do all things through Christ which strengtheneth me" (Philippians 4:13). Even though you are dealing with tribulation, you can have a smile on your face because you can overcome it. You are going to win because He has made winning available to you.

Look Up!

When you're going through trials and tribulations, which you may be right now, it's important where you have your focus. Satan will try to pull your focus toward him, but Psalm 121 says, "I will lift up mine eyes unto the hills, from whence cometh my help" (v. 1). Now, if the psalmist is saying he will lift up his eyes, he must not have been looking up in the first place. It is critical to get your eyes off your problem and on your answer.

God gave Abraham some amazing promises when he was old and gray. Abraham could have looked at his body and said, "No way, Lord," but he didn't. The Bible says he stopped looking at his body or his wife's (Romans 4:19). Instead, he focused on what God said: that he would be the father of a great nation. He praised God for it, totally confident that God was going to do what He said He would. And God did it.

The Cavalry Is Here

"From whence cometh my help. My help cometh from the LORD, which made heaven and earth" (Psalm 121:1–2). Every time I meditate on these verses, I think about one of those old westerns where the cavalry came down the hill to save the day in spite of overwhelming odds. We are talking about the One who died for you; He is coming to help you—despite whatever overwhelming odds you face. Hebrews 4:16 says, "Come boldly unto the throne of grace, that we may obtain mercy, and find grace to help in time of need." Whatever you need right now, help is available from heaven. It comes right from heaven to you with these promises:

> He will not suffer thy foot to be moved: he that keepeth thee will not slumber. Behold, he that keepeth Israel shall neither slumber nor sleep. The LORD is thy keeper: the LORD is thy shade upon thy right hand. The sun shall not smite thee by day, nor the moon by night. The LORD shall preserve thee from all evil: he shall preserve thy soul. The LORD shall preserve thy going out and thy coming in from this time forth, and even for evermore.
>
> —PSALM 121:3–8

How can you read that and not have your faith built up? So stop being afraid that the trials you're facing are going to take you out. The last one didn't, and the one before that didn't, and the one before that didn't, and the one before that didn't. If God did it before, He doesn't change. He will do it again.

When Peter walked on the water, he took his eyes off Jesus and started to sink. When he fixed his eyes back on Jesus, he walked on water right back to the boat. You can win because Jesus has already overcome the world for you, but you've got to take your eyes off your problem and look up. Keep your eyes focused on Him. "Look not at the things which are seen, but at the things which are not seen: for the things which are seen are temporal; but the things which are not seen are eternal" (2 Corinthians 4:18). Stop being afraid of your problem. Be courageous, and keep your eyes on the One who told you that He has overcome the world.

Good God, Bad Devil

"The thief cometh not, but for to steal, and to kill, and to destroy: I am come that they might have life, and that they might have it more abundantly."

—JOHN 10:10

WHY DO BAD THINGS happen to good people? Why does God let you go through hurts? Why is life so hard? Today we are going to answer these questions and get a godly perspective on them. In doing so, we will tackle one of the greatest lies on Earth that prevents millions of people from knowing God. Hopefully, you have not bought into this lie.

We live in a world where terrible things happen to people all over the world. Every day, we hear about another natural disaster. We turn on the television and see little children in Africa dying from hunger. Innocent people are murdered every week. You might have lost a child. You might have been brought up in a home where you were abused. You might have been raped or gone through financial ruin. Who is to blame for these tragedies? That is the question we're going to answer today.

I heard a well-known talk-show hostess rant and rave about God: "If God was real, if God was so good, then why are there hurricanes? Why do children die? And why is there this? And why is there that?" She listed all the ills of the world and decided they were all God's fault. Here is the key: Because she felt like it was God's fault, there was no way she was going to receive Him, love Him, serve Him, or be blessed or used by Him.

That is the problem with blaming God. When you blame Him for what is going on in your life—instead of who is really to blame—you turn away from Him instead of toward Him. And the results are disastrous. You might be saying, "I'd never blame God for bad things happening," but you could be doing it unknowingly. When someone passes away at an early age, for example, do you say, "The Lord needed another piano player in heaven"? Or "He needed another voice in the choir"? Or "God must have wanted him in heaven more than He needed him on Earth"? Or the blanket phrase, "It was God's will"?

If you're going through a pressure-cooker situation, as we all do from time to time, do you say, "God, I love You. I'm one of Your children. I've been serving You. I've been giving my time. So why did You let this happen?" Maybe you quote Job: "The LORD gave, and the LORD hath taken away" (Job 1:21). Job said a lot of things that weren't right. Everything in the Bible is truth, but not everything said by people in the Bible is true.

Let's settle once and for all who is really to blame for the ills of the world. The world says God is to blame—but the Word says the Devil is to blame.

We're going to look at a number of Scripture verses that prove this. Let's start with Jesus sharing the parable of the sower: "The sower soweth the word. And these are they by the way side, where the word is sown; but when they have heard, Satan cometh immediately, and taketh away the word that was sown in their hearts" (Mark 4:14–15).

If God is the one who sent the Word to you so that it could produce something good in your life, then why would God send affliction and persecution against you so that the Word won't work? It doesn't even make sense, yet that's what so many people believe. Jesus said, "The thief cometh not, but for to steal, and to kill, and to destroy: I am come that they might have life, and that they might have it more abundantly" (John 10:10). The Devil comes to steal your health, your peace of mind, your money, your children, and whatever else he can get his hands on to take from you. Jesus warned you that the Devil comes to kill—that he wants to end your life. That doesn't sound good to me. That sounds like evil. In fact, let me clue you in on something. If you take the word *God* and add a letter *o* to it, what would you get? The word *good*. Now take the word *evil* and add a letter *d* to it, and what do you get? *Devil*. So if it is good, it is from God. If it is evil, it is from the Devil.

When Jesus knew He was about to be crucified, He prayed to His Father, "Keep them from the evil" (John 17:15). Why would He ask His Father to protect them from evil if He were doing the evil? God is good. The Devil is evil.

Paul says, "Put on the whole armour of God, that ye may be able to stand against the wiles of the devil" (Ephesians 6:11). If God were bringing trials and temptations into your life, why would Paul tell you to resist them? Why would he tell you that God gave you armor if you are supposed to use that armor to fight God? No. God says put on your armor and use it so that you can be protected against the Devil. God is good. The Devil is evil.

Misguided Christians love to talk about Paul's thorn in the flesh, saying God sent sickness and disease to keep him humble. But Paul said it was a "messenger of Satan to buffet [him]" (2 Corinthians 12:7). Paul never said God gave him the thorn. God is good. The Devil is evil.

God warns us, "Be sober, be vigilant; because your adversary the devil, as a roaring lion, walketh about, seeking whom he may devour" (1 Peter 5:8). He didn't say, "Your

There was no evil in the world until the Devil showed up.

adversary, God." Why would God warn you to be vigilant if He Himself were bringing harm? God is good. The Devil is evil.

What Happens When You Blame God, Not the Devil

Can you see why the Devil tries so hard to make you believe he isn't responsible for evil? He wants you to blame God! Remember the passage in Mark 4 that we looked at earlier? "When affliction or persecution ariseth for the word's sake, immediately they are offended" (v. 17). The Amplified Bible says they are "displeased, indignant, resentful." At whom? At God! If you believe that God, not the Devil, is behind bad things that happen to you, you actually get offended at Him and it causes the Word not to produce fruit in your life.

Something else happens when you blame God for bad things happening: You don't take responsibility for your own actions. There is a principle in the earth called "seed time and harvest," meaning you plant a seed and then you harvest what grows from it. You make a choice, and there are consequences that result from it. If you've consistently used your credit card to run up debt, for example, and now the bank is repossessing your car to pay for it all, you can't blame God for that. It's seed time and harvest—you planted financial mismanagement, and now you've reaped the harvest.

We need to understand exactly who the Devil is. Jesus called him a thief whose mission statement is "to steal, and to kill, and to destroy" (John 10:10). There was no evil in the world until the Devil showed up. In Genesis, when God created the world, it was perfect. God gave man dominion over the fish of the sea, the fowl of the air, over all the earth, and told him to subdue it. When the Devil showed up, Adam could have said to him, "Die right now," because God had already given him all authority. Instead, Adam bought the Devil's lie and sinned, thus handing the lease to Satan.

So you are now living on a planet where Satan has been in control. The kingdom of darkness has covered the earth, but because of Jesus, you have a new covenant with God. Every time you tell someone about Jesus and they get saved, the light spreads further, pushing back the darkness until the day comes and the earth will be filled with the glory of God once again.

We have the wrong guy on trial. We've got God up on the stand, and we are trying Him for what He is supposedly doing in our lives while the real murderer is running loose. There is a madman out there—a serial killer who is stealing, killing, and destroying—and we are shaking our fist at God instead of recognizing that the enemy is the Devil and that God gave you complete authority over him.

Let's end today with this true-or-false test.

1. God is responsible for kids starving in Africa. Is that true or false? It is false. God loves children and states in Matthew 18 that if you mistreat one, you will face great judgment. Surely He doesn't mistreat them.

2. God causes evil circumstances to teach you something. Is that true or false? False. God does not use Satan's tools to teach you His lessons. He doesn't make you sick or poor, and He doesn't make someone die to teach you something. Jesus said, "The Comforter, which is the Holy Ghost, whom the Father will send in my name, he shall teach you all things" (John 14:26).

3. God causes evil circumstances to develop your character. True or false? False. If God sent sickness to teach you something, aren't you out of the will of God when you go to the doctor to get rid of it? If He sent financial trouble your way to develop your character, aren't you wrong to get a job? What develops your character is the Word of God and steadfastly acting on that Word in the midst of your trouble.

God didn't send any of these evils your way. In fact, read Psalm 91 to see how He actually protects you from evil. The Lord is good, and His mercy endures forever. He will take what Satan meant for evil and will turn it to your good. God is not your problem. He is your answer.

Day 5

Your Turn

Thus saith the LORD of hosts; Turn ye unto me, saith the LORD of hosts, and I will turn unto you, saith the LORD of hosts.

—ZECHARIAH 1:3

As you're going through our twenty-eight-day challenge, I'm sure there are very specific ways you want God to be directly involved in particular aspects of your life, whether it's your marriage, your children, your finances, your career, your health, or some other important area that you listed on day one. You want something supernatural to happen. You know God wants greater things for you than what the world has to offer, but perhaps you don't know how to tap into that. How do you win?

Zechariah 1:3 provides a good answer to that question. God says, "Turn to Me and I will turn to you." Can it really be that simple? If you've ever played chess or checkers, you know the other player makes a move and then it's your move. God has already made His move. God has already done what He needs to do. His power is poised to provide for you. He's ready to go ahead and make the next move but He needs you to do your part. It's your turn.

We can learn four things from this passage in Zechariah.

1. Whether or not the people turned to God was entirely up to them. God put it in their hands, but it was their choice to respond or not. He says, "You turn to me. You are the one who is going to decide whether or not this happens."

2. God told them to turn, implying they had their back turned to Him and were turned away.

3. Turning to Him means turning away from some other things. In those days, it was probably false gods. In our day, it could mean drugs, sex, the wrong lifestyle, alcohol, addictions, or other things that might be gods to us.

4. God, too, was turned away from them. Notice He says, "And I will turn to you." If you turn to Him, He will turn to you. I don't know about you, but I don't want God turned away from me. I want God to turn to me, because I know if He does, good things are going to happen in my life.

So it really is up to you. It's your move. You can ask, "God, why didn't this happen in my life?" but you forget that He has already done His part. He's already made available everything that needs to be made available for you to succeed. It's now up to you.

You know God wants greater things for you than what the world has to offer, but perhaps you don't know how to tap into that.

Plug It In

My iPhone comes with a little charger. If I want to charge the phone, I plug the charger into the outlet and then plug the phone into the charger. All of a sudden, the power in the outlet gets to the iPhone. God is like the outlet. Because Jesus chose to be the mediator, you can get hooked up with God. Until that point, you didn't have access to His power and all He could provide for you, but because of the mediator named Jesus, now you can be charged up with everything God has for you.

Ephesians 1:3 says, "Blessed be the God and Father of our Lord Jesus Christ, who hath blessed us with all spiritual blessings in heavenly places in Christ." Notice the past tense here. God has already blessed you with every spiritual blessing. Now that you are a child of God, you're in a covenant with the almighty God, and every spiritual blessing belongs to you.

Let's say you are a parent and you have made a lot of sacrifices to put your daughter in a particular school. Maybe she loves the arts, and you spent a lot of time and money working toward getting her accepted into the right school. You pay the tuition. You pay for the dorm room. You pay for everything your child needs. You walk her into the classroom and you say, "Now it is up to you. I've done everything. It's your turn." That's what God has done for you.

Let's Apply It

Let's look at some areas where you can apply this to your life.

1. The presence of God. "Draw nigh to God, and he will draw nigh to you" (James 4:8). I like the idea of God coming closer to me. In His presence is fullness of joy, right? When He shows up, that is when good things happen in my life. You may have heard about practicing the presence of God, and this is where it begins. Draw close to Him—it's your move.

2. Friendship with God. Genesis 5:22 says, "Enoch walked with God." It doesn't say, "And God walked with Enoch," because then it would read as if God just chose Enoch. The choice was Enoch's. He chose to walk with God. The Amplified Bible says he walked in "habitual fellowship." It was his habit to fellowship with God. That doesn't mean he just had a Sunday morning hookup with Him. It wasn't just a prayer date once or twice a week. This is how he lived—in habitual fellowship. The Knox Bible translation says he lived as "God's close friend." Paul wrote about the "communion of the Holy Ghost" (2 Corinthians 13:14). The Message Bible calls it the "intimate friendship of the Holy Spirit." When you are talking to God throughout the day and He's talking to you throughout the day, you are truly walking with God. Isn't that what you'd love? If you want to experience a deeper friendship with Him in your daily life, then it is up to you. Turn to Him, and He will turn to you.

3. The kingdom of God. If you want more of the kingdom of God in your life and less influence from the kingdom of the Devil, you can have it. It's your turn. "Seek ye first the kingdom of God" (Matthew 6:33). It begins with you seeking. That means you put your attention on the kingdom of God. You put your passion into it. Colossians 3:2 says, "Set your affection on things above, not on things on the earth." God says, "You do that, and all these thing will be added" (Matthew 6:33). It's a promise. One of the definitions of the word *added* is "annexed." It is literally attached you.

4. Wisdom. James 1:5 says, "If any of you lack wisdom, let him ask... it shall be given to him." In times of trouble, you need wisdom. You need to know what to do. The good news is that God gives it freely, but notice that He gives it to you when you ask. You do your part, and then God gives wisdom to you.

5. Knowing God's plan for your life. God doesn't want to hide His plan from you. If you don't know what God has called you to do, that's not God's fault; it's yours! I love you, but I am being straight with you because at some point you have to get to that revelation. You can't keep saying, "I am waiting on God to tell me." Five years pass and you still say, "I am just waiting on the Lord to tell me." Ten years pass. If you don't know what God has called you to do, it is because you haven't sought Him like the Bible says. It is up to you.

In our church's youth department, our goal is that our young people do not finish youth ministry without knowing what God has called them to do. It's very simple. You ask Him, believing you receive God's plan for you at that moment. Then you continue to seek Him in prayer daily concerning it until you get quiet enough to hear from Him about it. You stay in that place until He shows you. He can't require you to do something if He hasn't told you what it is. The burden is not on Him to tell you because He is ready and willing. It's on you to seek Him out and ask.

6. Direction for your future. The Bible says, "In all thy ways acknowledge him, and he shall direct they paths" (Proverbs 3:6). You turn to Him, and He will direct your paths. That is a promise. It's like spending time on the Internet looking for an answer. It's there—you just have to search for it until you find it. You want to know God's direction for your future? Turn toward Him. He is there all along. You just need to spend some time in prayer. Turn off the TV at night and get up a little earlier and go spend some time with God in prayer. He'll give you the answers that you need for your life.

It's your turn. It's your move.

Day 6

Shake Yourself

Samson...awoke out of his sleep, and said, "I will go out as at other times before, and shake myself."

—JUDGES 16:20

O F ALL THE PEOPLE we read about in the Bible, Samson was certainly one of the strongest and most victorious on whatever battlefield he faced. Today we're going to learn about his secret— and how you can apply it to win in the battles you face.

In Judges 16, Delilah warns Samson that the Philistines are just around the corner, ready to attack. Can't you just see him shrugging his shoulders and saying, "No problem. I'm going to go handle this the same way I've handled it many times before"? How did he handle danger or attacks against him in the past? When he faced a lion, "the Spirit of the LORD came mightily upon him, and he rent him as he would have rent a kid [tear it apart], and he had nothing in his hand" (Judges 14:6). Later we read, "And the Spirit of the LORD came upon him, and he went down to Ashkelon, and slew thirty men of them" (14:19). And again, "When he came unto Lehi, the Philistines shouted against him: and the Spirit of the LORD came mightily upon him.... And he found a new jawbone of an ass, and put forth his hand, and took it, and slew a thousand men therewith" (15:14, 15). Do you see a pattern here? *The Spirit of the Lord came upon him. The Spirit of the Lord came upon him. The Spirit of the Lord came upon him.*

So when Delilah came with another report of another attack, we have some insight into how Samson approached threats: "I will go out

43

as at other times before, and shake myself." That is a strange opening of Scripture, isn't it? A lot of translations say "shake myself free," but there was nothing for him to shake himself free from. If you study the word *shake* here, it has the idea of the rustling of a mane, which usually accompanies a lion's roar. A lion shakes his mane and roars as a way of asserting his dominance over his territory.

When Samson got the bad report, he didn't cower. He didn't get afraid. He didn't take on a victim mentality: "Oh, why do they continue to attack me? Oh me. Poor me." No. He ran out to face his enemies, and he shook his mane like he was ready to fight. He was doing much more than just asserting his dominance here; he was getting ready for the power of God to move. He was not backing away from the attack. He was coming at the attack. The Philistines weren't going to happen to him—he was about to happen to the Philistines.

Of course, by this point in Samson's life, we know he had already sinned, but in the past this is what he would do. He would shake himself and then he would have victory—and that's the point I want you to grasp today. You may be under attack yourself. It may not be the Philistines who are coming at you, but it may be sickness, financial trouble, or marital problems. If you're not careful, you can cower and take on a victim mentality:

When God wants to crush Satan, He uses you to do it! You're His Satan-crushing tool.

"Oh me, oh my." You can act like you're helpless, when in reality you have available to you exactly what Samson had: the very power of God. You need to get rid of the victim mentality. Stop worrying about why this keeps happening to you, and instead say, "You know what? Thanks be to God, who always causes me to triumph. In all these things, I am more than a conqueror." Shake yourself and get ready to use the power of God to knock the Devil out. Use your God-given power so that the Enemy will be defeated.

A few days ago in this twenty-eight-day challenge, we learned who is behind every trial and temptation: the Devil. Ephesians 6 makes this very clear. If you are going to be victorious, you have to deal with the root—the Devil himself. The good news is that God has given you the authority to do so. Jesus gave His disciples authority and power over Satan and sent them out to minister. They came back to Him amazed at what happened: "And the seventy returned again with joy, saying, Lord, even the devils are subject unto us through thy name" (Luke 10:17). Every demon spirit had to bow before them because of the authority Jesus gave them. Jesus went on to tell them, "I beheld Satan as lightning fall from heaven. Behold, I give unto you power to tread on serpents and scorpions, and over all the power of the enemy: and nothing shall by any means hurt you" (vv. 18–19). The word *power* means "authority."

I was meditating on that one day, and I realized I had underlined only the words "I give unto you power," but I hadn't underlined "to tread." I suddenly understood that Jesus Himself was giving me authority to walk on and dominate Satan. Romans 16:20 says, "God...will soon crush Satan under your feet" (NIV). When God wants to crush Satan, He uses you to do it! You're His Satan-crushing tool. Notice in Luke that Jesus calls these demon spirits "serpents and scorpions." Where do you usually see these animals crawling? On the ground. So Jesus has given you authority to tread on them, to walk on them, and ultimately to crush and destroy them—all of them. He says "all the power of the enemy." That means you have authority over all the power that the Enemy has—everything the Devil has, meaning every trick, every spell, every curse. Whatever he has is under your feet. It can't work on you. You have authority, and as long as you decide to use that authority, it won't work on you.

Jesus takes it even further when He says, "And nothing shall by any means hurt you." That means no weapon formed against you shall prosper. No evil shall befall you. The weapon might be formed. It might be aimed. It might be fired. It might be *this close* to hitting you, but when it gets to that point, it is going to fall apart right in front of you because God's Word promises that nothing by any means shall hurt you. Just because you are in danger of losing something doesn't mean you are going to lose it. It does mean God is going to move mightily. You will dominate in that situation if you use your authority. God will back you up.

You need to treat the Devil like you treat the flies that get into your house. When we were growing up, my dad didn't mind the flies being outside, but when even one got inside the house and was flying around the kitchen table, he got out the flyswatter and went after it. He wasn't happy until he found it. It could be missing for thirty minutes and he'd be on a hunt all over the house looking for it, turning on the light in one room and turning off all the other lights in the house, trying to lure it into the light.

That's how you've got to be with the Devil when he tries to get in your house. The Bible warns you not give the Devil place. That means you have authority over your household. You don't have to let sickness, poverty, or addictions in. You have authority. Shake yourself and use it. "Be strong in the Lord, and in the power of his might" (Ephesians 6:10).

"The wicked flee when no man pursueth: but the righteous are bold as a lion" (Proverbs 28:1). Lions are not shy. Have you ever seen a video of a lion in Africa? He walks wherever he wants to. He is completely bold because he knows something: He is the baddest thing out there. He knows by experience that anybody who tries to challenge him gets eaten. He is completely bold. The Word of God tells you that as a Christian, you also ought to be bold. This is part of what it means to be strong in the power of His might. When you put on the armor of God and are doing what God's Word says, you can be bold in doing it—and God will back you up. So shake yourself and go tread on some demons.

I Can Win

1. What did you read during this section that surprised you or challenged you?

_____

_____

_____

_____

_____

_____

2. What did you think about your ability to be victorious before you started this challenge?

_____

_____

_____

_____

_____

_____

_____

3. Briefly describe what God is saying to you now about your ability to be victorious. This will probably change throughout the twenty-eight days, but write as much as you know now.

_____

_____

_____

_____

_____

_____

_____

_____

_____

4. Quote two Scriptures, one from the Old Testament and one from the New Testament, that prove God has already given you the power to be victorious.

_____

_____

_____

_____

_____

5. List Scripture verses here that God has quickened to you during the past six days. Use them as declarations during the next week to remind yourself of God's promises that you can win and be victorious, no matter what you face.

_____

_____

_____

_____

_____

_____

_____

_____

6. Update the victory pages you filled out on day one (and continue updating them throughout the twenty-eight-day challenge). In which areas are you beginning to see victory?

_____

_____

_____

_____

_____

_____

_____

Step 2:

GO THROUGH

Day 7

No Parking

Though I walk through the valley of the shadow of death...

—Psalm 23:4

Psalm 23 is a popular Scripture to read at funerals, but in reality, this psalm is not about heaven. It's about life here on Earth before we get to heaven. There are no "valleys of the shadow of death," "evil," or "enemies" in heaven. Psalm 23 is about life in the here and now. Today we will look at verse 4—a verse we don't like to read. I mean, be honest. Don't you love the idea of lying down in green pastures by still waters? Don't you love the thought of feasting at banqueting tables? Who wants to think about going through the valley of the shadow of death to get there?

You know that God wants to prosper you, but as I've already mentioned, if you are not careful, you can easily conclude that a prosperous life is one where you never face any difficulties. That's not what the Bible says. The prosperous life is a victorious life. You prosper because you overcome the Enemy. Although the Lord is your Shepherd, you are going to go through seasons when you are under attack. If this book is about winning, then there has to be a battle that you win. The obstacles and difficulties are part of it. If you are not careful, you will get offended at God because you are in the valley—but the valleys are not God's fault. They are just a fact of life on Planet Earth. Please remember what we learned on day four regarding who is responsible for evil—it's not God.

Now for the good news. Note that the psalmist did not say, "You're going to encounter valleys of the shadow of death." He said you would go *through* them. The word I want you to focus on today is *through*. You don't have to park there in the valley of the shadow of death because you're going through it.

Tiffany and I were watching the summer Olympics a few years ago and were amazed when the winner of the marathon finished the race in less than two hours. That's twenty-six miles! My wife and I are pretty athletic. We both played basketball beyond high school and try to stay in decent shape, yet we looked at the winner and thought, "You have got to be in tremendous shape to run twenty-six miles and do it under two hours."

A marathon is a grueling race, yet it's over in a few hours. Going through the valley of the shadow of death can be grueling too—and it's usually not over in two hours. Sometimes you are in that valley for a while. You don't go in one day and come out the next. Sometimes you are in the midst of an attack for a while—but what you do when you're in the valley determines how quickly you will go through it and what kind of shape you will be in when you come out.

Another word we can use for the valley is *wilderness*. There are wild beasts in the wilderness, and I'm not talking about rabid dogs. There are lions, tigers, and bears, oh my. The wilderness can be a dangerous place.

Let's look at some of the reasons you end up in this place. Sometimes you go through the valley simply because you are attacked. We tell students who enroll in our school of ministry to be prepared because the minute they get in the Word of God, Satan is going to attack them. Some of them look at us like we're crazy, but a month later, they see what we're talking about. Folks are losing their jobs, and Satan is attacking left and right—and it is simply because they are getting in the Word and God is taking them somewhere the Devil doesn't want them to go. (See Mark 4:15.) Thank God that when the school year ends, they are able to rejoice and say, "Look what the Lord has done." It didn't matter what Satan tried to do. They come through and God prospers them.

Sometimes the Spirit of the Lord actually leads you into the valley. This isn't something we want to believe, but it's in the Word—and it happened to Jesus: "And Jesus being full of the Holy Ghost returned from Jordan, and was led by the Spirit into the wilderness" (Luke 4:1). God sent Him into the wilderness. Why? Because sometimes you have to go through the valley to get to the future God has for you. God sent the children of Israel through the wilderness on the way to the Promised Land. God told Abraham to leave his family and everything he knew and get on the road. In fact, God didn't even tell Abraham where he was going until he got on the road. Do you think that was convenient? Do you think maybe Abraham caught some stuff from his family? And what about Isaiah? Be thankful God didn't tell you to take your clothes off and walk around for three years almost naked just a make a point. I don't know about you, but if God told me that, at the end of three years I would be saying, "God, You could have gotten a doll and made it naked. I could have walked around and shown everybody the doll, and we could have accomplished the same purpose."

Sometimes you end up in the valley because of your own actions and choices. Psalm 107:17–18 says, "Fools because of their transgression, and because of their iniquities, are afflicted. Their soul abhorreth all manner of meat; and they draw near unto the gates of death." Sometimes you get in trouble because you sinned. You put yourself there. The good news is that even if you missed it, you can go before God, repent of that sin, and God will forgive you and bring restoration to your life so that whatever was lost can be restored to you and your future.

Notice that it's not the "valley of death" but the "valley of the shadow of death." A shadow never hurt anybody.

Don't Park the Car There

Whatever reason you are in the valley of the shadow of death, I want you to keep your eyes on the word *through*. That is a faith confession right there. In the natural, you may be thinking, "If I go in, I may not come out." There is a reason it is called the shadow of death—because some folk go to die there. You, however, can say by the Spirit of God, "I am going *through*. God is not expecting me to go in that valley and get taken out. I'm not getting taken out by bankruptcy or cancer or divorce. I'm not going to lose my kids. I may be in the valley, but I am not staying here. God is bringing me *through* the valley, and I am going to come out—and I am going to come out victorious."

Notice that it's not the "valley of death" but the "valley of the shadow of death." A shadow never hurt anybody. The shadow of death is all Satan has. If he could take you out, he would have already done it. The only way he can get you is if you let him. All he can do is try to put pressure on you and try to scare you into believing, "I am going to fail." But the psalmist says, "Yea, though I walk through the valley of the shadow of death; I will fear no evil." He's made a decision: "I will." And he gives the reason why he doesn't have to fear any evil: "I will fear no evil: for thou art with me; thy rod and thy staff they comfort me" (Psalm 23:4). God's shepherd's rod and staff are there to comfort and protect. A rod is a weapon that the shepherd uses to punish any animal that comes to take the sheep. So the psalmist says, "I know, God, that if the enemy comes against me, You will use Your rod to smash him." You as a believer are His rod now. God has given you authority. The staff is something the shepherd would hold up and the sheep could see it from a distance. By following his staff, they knew where to go. So the psalmist is saying, "God, I know You will guide me out of trouble. I believe there is a way through this. I believe You know the way through it and that You will guide me right through it."

Remember the three Hebrew young men? Shadrach, Meshach, and Abednego were thrown into a fiery furnace that was so hot, the men who threw them in died. Yet when they came out, not only were they alive but their clothes didn't even smell of smoke. It was as if they never went in—except that when they came out, they had such a mighty testimony that even the king became a believer in God.

It's the same with you. The wilderness can be a no-parking zone for you. You will go *through* the valley of the shadow of death. And if you keep your eyes on Him, when you come out, it will be glorious.

Day 8

Detour

"I will restore to you the years that the locust hath eaten."

—JOEL 2:25

I LOVE OUR VERSE TODAY. I love the fact that God says, "I will," because any time God says, "I will," you can take it to the bank. If He says that to you, He is going to do it. He is not a God who lies or changes His mind. If He says it, He will perform it. If you need something restored, it means something that belonged to you has been lost. Think about the areas you listed at the beginning of our twenty-eight-day challenge—areas where you need to win and see victory. How many of those are areas where something needs to be restored—either your health, your finances, family members, a job, or something else? These are areas where the Enemy was able to get in and steal what God intended you to have.

You serve a God who is in the business of restoring to you what the Enemy has taken from you. Notice that He says, "I will restore to you the years." He didn't say, "Some of the years." He didn't say, "I'll restore to you everything you lost in the last thirty days." No, He says, "I am going to restore to you everything you lost during all those years that you were under attack and even everything you lost during all those years you messed up. I'm restoring all of it to you."

Now, you could ask why Scriptures like this are even in the Bible. Why do you need restoration? The answer is because sometimes in life, you end up on a detour from the plan of God for your life. It may be because of something that someone else did to you. It may be something you did your-self. Or maybe there were things entirely out of your control. Whatever the reason, you were following God's plan for life, and somewhere along the line, instead of getting right to where God wanted you to be, you ended up on a detour. You were no longer heading toward the place God had for you. You ended up on a detour.

No one likes detours. I certainly don't. When we lived in Georgia, sometimes we would gather up the kids, jump in the car, and drive down to Orlando. If you are driving in the car with little kids for hours on end, you want to get there as quickly as you can. Normally it's about a seven-hour drive, but sometimes, all of a sudden, we would see the dreaded signs— cars slowing down and turning off the interstate onto some backwoods road. *Detour!* We'd started out on a nice, smooth interstate but suddenly found ourselves in the middle of nowhere with no idea how long it would take to get where we were heading.

The good thing about hitting a detour is that eventually the road signs will point the way to get you back on track—and finally you get where you wanted to go all along. It's the same way for our journey with God. He is not surprised that you ended up on a detour. He doesn't say, "Wow, I didn't know *that* was going to happen." He knew all along that you would be trying to live this life and that certain things would happen to cause you to get away from where He wanted you to be. So He always has a Plan B in place to get you back on track.

Today, you're going learn how to navigate through a detour and get back on track so that you can fulfill God's plan for your life.

Board the Ship

We'll begin by looking at one of Paul's journeys. Even though Paul was once the chief persecutor of the early church, when God got hold of him, he became one of the chief missionaries of it. God's plan was for Paul to take the Gospel to the Jews, Gentiles, and finally to kings (Acts 9:15). Later in his life, he went before governors, kings, and others in positions of high authority. Finally God put it on his heart to go see the man who was king over the greatest kingdom on the planet at that time—Caesar. It was the plan of God for Paul to go to Rome and stand before Caesar. Yet at the beginning of this particular journey, Paul was in prison. Still, that didn't stop the plan of God from unfolding. That was just one of the detours Paul encountered along the way.

Let's begin in Acts 27. Paul and the others boarded the ship and made their first stop at a port called Fair Havens. And here's where things began to go downhill:

> Now when much time was spent, and when sailing was now dangerous, because the fast was now already past, Paul admonished them, and said unto them, Sirs, I perceive that this voyage will be with hurt and much damage, not only of the lading and ship, but also of our lives. Nevertheless the centurion believed the master and the owner of the ship, more than those things which were spoken by Paul.
>
> —vv. 9–11

If you've ever been on a cruise, you know there are certain times of the year you do not want to be at sea. In the South, we call it hurricane season. There are certain seasons in the Mediterranean where storms come up, too, and Paul knew by the Holy Ghost that if they sailed then, they would suffer great damage. He warned the others, but they didn't listen to him. And just as Paul prophesied, there was a tremendous storm resulting in a shipwreck with "much damage."

When you face a storm in your own life, you've got to look past it and find God's Word for you in it.

Yet all was not lost. An angel of the Lord appeared to Paul, saying, "Fear not, Paul; thou must be brought before Caesar: and, lo, God hath given thee all them that sail with thee" (v. 24). Paul was so encouraged that he could say to the others caught in this disaster, "Be of good cheer: for I believe God, that it shall be even as it was told me" (v. 25). And of course it was. Eventually, he arrived at Rome because the plan of God will always come to pass.

Reverse the Call

In 2010, a Detroit Tigers pitcher named Armando Galarraga was just one out away from pitching a perfect game. There have only been twenty-one perfect games in the history of Major League Baseball, and never one in Detroit Tigers' history. Galarraga got to the last inning and made the right pitch. The batter hit the ball, a Tiger player caught it and threw it to first base, and the baseman caught it. The player should have been out. We should have been celebrating because the guy was clearly out—yet the umpire called him safe. Later on, the umpire admitted he messed up. He cost Galarraga a perfect game and a place in the history books. Major League Baseball said they would not reverse the call.

The good news is that God will always reverse the call for you. God can play the clock back. God, unlike Major League Baseball, can reverse the decision. He can make it right for you if you follow His plan. He's got a plan to get you back from wherever the detour took you. When the angel showed up and reminded Paul that God's plan was to get him before Caesar, it didn't matter what detour Paul was on. Paul knew God was going to do whatever He had to do to get him back on track so that he could get where he was supposed to be. Once Paul heard from God, he could see past the storm. He could see past the bad call. He could see himself going to Rome despite storms and shipwrecks. He could have chosen to continue looking at the storm, but he said, "I choose to believe God."

When you face a storm in your own life, you've got to look past it and find God's Word for you in it. Then you must remember what God said to you in the middle of that storm. You have to see the future God has for you instead of seeing yourself sinking and drowning. Sinking and drowning is not part of God's plan for you. Being taken out is not part of God's plan for you. God's plan is that you overcome whatever you are dealing with right now. God's plan is that you go through the storm and are able to say, "Yeah, I was walking through the valley of the shadow of death, but the Lord was with me. His rod and His staff comforted me. He made a table for me in the presence of my enemies." That is the plan of God for you.

So look up. Look at the hills from which cometh your help. Look to the almighty God. Remember who you serve. Remember that you belong to Him. Remember what He said to you, and go forward believing God that you will come out of this victorious.

I personally believe that Paul did not go through fourteen days of one of the worst experiences of his life without praying. The worst sinner on the earth in this situation would start praying. They may not even know who they are praying to, but they'd be praying. When you face a detour, in order to know God's plan for you, you have to take the time to hear from God. James said, "If any of you lack wisdom, let him ask of God.... But let him ask in faith, nothing wavering" (James 1:5, 6). That's talking about going through hard times. God has a word for you, just like He had a word for Paul, and it will help you to be strong and go through.

Detours are a part of this life here on Earth—in the natural and spiritual. And there are seven points I want to highlight for you today as you think about the detours in your own life.

1. Look past the storm. Take the time to hear God in the midst of the storm. Focus on the future God has for you.

2. Be patient. In the midst of the storm, God spoke to Paul that everything would be all right, but the circumstances didn't turn around immediately—at least not on the timetable I would have chosen if I were in the middle of a hurricane. Don't give God a deadline.

3. Have faith in God. Be like Paul and encourage yourself in the Lord, "I believe what was said to me. I believe what the Word says. I believe God is a God who makes a way in the wilderness."

4. Be of good cheer. That's not rocket science, is it? Cheer up. Wherever there is faith, there is joy. If there is no joy, there is no faith. Get back in the Word of God, and stir up the joy of the Lord on the inside of you.

5. Be a blessing. When they finally made landfall, Paul could have sulked in a corner, but instead he prayed for the sick, and so many were healed that a healing revival broke out (Acts 28:8–9).

6. Treat other people right. Paul never mistreated anyone, even those who mistreated him. That doesn't mean he didn't seek justice, but he treated people right.

7. Repent where you missed it. If you are the one who caused your own detour, you may need to get before God, repent, and ask for His forgiveness. Like the father in the story of the prodigal son, your heavenly Father will be waiting with open arms to welcome you, forgive you, restore what was stolen from you, and set you back on the path to fulfilling His purposes for your life.

Whatever detours you face in your walk with God, if you follow these seven points, you will end up like Paul, saying, "I have fought a good fight, I have finished my course, I have kept the faith" (2 Timothy 4:7).

Day 9

Take Two

"But the LORD thy God turned the curse into a blessing unto thee."

—DEUTERONOMY 23:5

L ET'S SAY YOU'RE IN a movie. In fact, let's make you the star of the film. As an actor or actress, you've always followed the script—until one day you decide you're not going to follow it anymore. You veer away from the dialogue and start making up your own lines. You're no longer following the script, and you're not even playing the character as the author intended. The director of the film sees what you're doing, but he doesn't fire you. He loves you and loves the movie and wants to make sure it turns out exactly as he planned. So he says, "Take two. I'm going to give you a second chance to get it right."

In life, the character you're really supposed to be playing is Christ in you, but let's face it—we can all say we have not totally, 100 percent of the time revealed the One living on the inside of us. Our "take one" wasn't too good, but we have a great Director, and He gets up in front of the world and says, "Take two. You get a second chance. You can do this thing all over again. You can get it right this time, and you can still get back on track for what I have for you."

He is the God of the second chance. You may have messed up big time, and you may be living with some of the consequences. There are things in your life that Satan meant for evil, but God is able to turn them around and bless you in the midst of it. In Deuteronomy 23, God spoke to the nation of Israel and reminded them of the time when Balaam was hired to declare a curse over them so that he could kill them and chase them out of the land. When the Bible talks about a curse, it is talking about an empowerment to fail. Instead of Israel receiving a curse, however, here's what happened: "Nevertheless the LORD thy God would not hearken unto Balaam; but the LORD thy God turned the curse into a blessing unto thee" (v. 5). God took the curse and turned it into a blessing. A blessing of the Lord is an empowerment to prosper.

Earlier in this study, we learned that we should not blame God for negative things that we may experience in life, that He is not responsible for them but will always make the best of a bad situation. He will take whatever the Enemy meant for evil and will turn it to your good. He will take the curse and turn it into a blessing. He will give you a second chance, a "take two."

There are things in your life that Satan meant for evil, but God is able to turn them around and bless you in the midst of it.

Now, God doesn't just automatically flip the switch for this to happen. You have to do your part. Remember yesterday when we looked at the seven points to remember as we go through life's detours? The seventh one was "Repent where you missed it." We all mess up, but thank God that is not the end of the story. "If we say that we have no sin, we deceive ourselves, and the truth is not in us. If we confess our sins, he is faithful and just to forgive us our sins, and to cleanse us from all unrighteousness" (1 John 1:8–9). The word *confess* means "to acknowledge." The Bible tells us that sin comes with a paycheck. "The wages of sin is death" (Romans 6:23), but Jesus paid that price. He is the propitiation for your sins. His blood gave God the right to forgive you and wash away your sins. So if you confess your sins, He is faithful and just to forgive you. Right there is something for you to shout about! God is not holding your sins against you, but instead He has pardoned you. God has said, "You don't have to pay the penalty for that sin. You are free to go."

Not only is He faithful and just to forgive you, but He is also faithful and just to cleanse you. Notice those are two separate things in the Scripture.

He not only lets you out of debtors' prison, but He also expunges the record so that it will be as if it never was. If someone pulled up your record, that sin would not be there anymore. In fact, the Bible says He remembers your sin no more (Isaiah 43:25). Ten years from now, He will not go back in time and say, "I remember when she did this." No. As far as God is concerned, it never happened. You get a "take two."

Sometimes this is difficult for Christians to grasp, especially if they've been walking with God for many years faithfully on the right path. Let's say you suddenly hit a detour and it's hard for you to believe God really forgives you and sets you back on the path again. You are so embarrassed that you run from God instead of running to Him. You reason, "It's over. There is nothing left for me in God, except maybe to hang in there until Jesus comes back and hope He really gives me eternal life in the end." If that's how you think, you are wrong. It's certainly not how God thinks. He still has a plan for your life. He is always ready to forgive. He still offers you a "take two."

No matter what you have done, you can still win and be victorious at life. You can still live out days of prosperity and years of pleasures. You can still have a future where God uses you to do mighty things for Him. One day you can still stand before Him and hear Him say, "Well done, good and faithful servant." There will still be laid up for you a crown of righteousness because He is a God of a second chance.

The Enemy has been trying to tell you what you can't have and what you can't do because of what you did. I am pulling the covers off him today. I am pulling them back so that you understand who is saying that to you. That is not your God saying it. That is not your King. That is your Enemy because he is afraid of you. He understands that even when he has deceived you and you have fallen into sin, once you get out of that detour, not only can God continue to use you, but God will use you to help others who have fallen in the same area. God will take that same experience that you had and empower you to turn around and help someone else not do it or be restored to God, just like you were. How many people were addicted to drugs and God brought them out, and now what do they do? They help folks get out of being addicted to drugs. How many people fell into adultery and it blew up their lives, but now they turn around and help others recover from that very thing or not go into that area in the first place?

"The Lord thy God turned the curse into a blessing unto thee." Once God has restored you, He will empower you to help the world around you—and that is the last thing Satan wants. He sent that curse to take you out, but God took that curse and turned it into a blessing.

If that is your story, realize that God has got big plans for you. Take advantage of His offer for a second chance. Take Him up on your "take two."

Take Three

"Behold, when we come into the land, thou shalt bind this line of scarlet thread in the window."

—JOSHUA 2:18

YESTERDAY, WE STUDIED HOW God is the God of a second chance. He always gives you a "take two." I have news for you. If you need it, He is also the God of a "take three." And if you need it, He is the God of a "take four." He is the God who will give you chance after chance after chance—as many takes as you need.

I want to spend another day on this because it is so critical to our focus on winning. If you don't believe God will always give you another chance when you mess up, you'll run from Him instead of to Him. If Satan can get you to believe his lies that God will always remember what you did and hold it against you, he can keep you from winning in life. If, however, you follow the words of 1 John 1:9, you can win: "If we confess our sins, he is faithful and just to forgive us our sins, and to cleanse us from all unrighteousness." God will turn the curse into a blessing for you.

Today, we're going to look at three individuals in the Bible and see how God gave them another chance—and what they went on to be and do with their lives. All of them are mentioned in the genealogy of Jesus in Matthew 1:1–16. This is a list in chronological order of all Jesus' physical ancestors going all the way back to Abraham.

Now, if you and I were putting together a group of individuals to be Jesus' physical ancestors, we would probably choose those who have the purest blood. They would all be perfect, or about as perfect as you could be until Jesus comes back. Yet that is not the case with this list. Most genealogies in the Bible list fathers and sons: "Obed begat Jesse and Jesse begat David" and so forth, from father to son, father to son. Yet this genealogy of Jesus mentions four women. And three of them, in one way or another, got a second chance.

We'll start with verse 5: "And Salmon begat Booz of Rachab." We know these individuals as Boaz and Rahab. Rahab was not exactly someone you would expect to find in the lineage of Jesus. Some Bible scholars believe this is the same Rahab mentioned in Joshua 2; others don't. But even if she isn't the same, the point we're making today is still valid—because God gave Rahab a second chance. In Joshua 2:1, we learn something significant about Rahab: She was a harlot. In fact, whenever she's mentioned throughout Scripture, she's referred to as "Rahab the harlot."

This wasn't someone who just committed a sexual sin one time. This is how she lived. This is what she did. She was a prostitute. That, of course, is clearly wrong in God's eyes and was a sin then as it is today—yet God gave this woman the opportunity for a second chance. When Joshua sent two spies into Jericho, Rahab hid them and protected them from the king. They could have been killed if she hadn't done this. In exchange, she made them promise to protect her and her family when they returned to take the city. This was their plan to do that—they told her, "Behold, when we come into the land, thou shalt bind this line of scarlet thread in the window" (Joshua 2:18). When the spies saw that scarlet thread, they'd know which house she and her family were in and they could rescue them before destroying the city. This scarlet thread is a foreshadowing of the blood of Jesus to redeem, cleanse, and protect. You can look throughout the Bible and find the blood in every book; here is one of those representations of the blood cleansing someone from their sin.

Joshua kept his part of the bargain. When Israel took Jericho and the walls came crumbling down, Joshua said, "Go in and destroy everybody except Rahab and her family." They looked for the scarlet thread and rescued Rahab and her family. The Bible says that Joshua honored the agreement and that Rahab and her family lived among the nation of Israel for the rest of their lives. I can guarantee you that she didn't live among them as a harlot. God had given her a second chance, and she went from living a sin-filled life that leads to destruction to a life among God's people and quite possibly in the very lineage of Jesus. God gave her a "take two."

Another Chance

In the lineage of Jesus, we find another woman who got a second chance: "David the king begat Solomon of her that had been the wife of Urias" (Matthew 1:6). This woman isn't mentioned by name, but we know who she is: Bathsheba. Her story is chronicled in 2 Samuel 11–12. David was king but decided to stay home from the battlefield. One night he took a walk on the roof of the palace and saw Bathsheba taking a bath. Why she was taking a bath outside at that hour is something we don't even need to go into. David slept with her, and she became pregnant. Ultimately, he ordered her husband back to the front lines to make sure he was killed. Once husband number one was out of the picture, David married Bathsheba.

God could have chosen anyone in the lineage of His only Son, and He chose to show His redemptive powers.

It was deception upon deception, and God sent the prophet Nathan to David to tell him exactly what he did wrong—and that the baby would die. The baby did die, but that is not the end of the story. God gave them both a second chance. David confessed his sin. He and Bathsheba had another child, Solomon, who went on to become one of Israel's greatest kings. Bathsheba became not just the wife of a king, but also the mother of a king—and she is in the lineage of Jesus.

Talk about a second chance! God could have chosen anyone in the lineage of His only Son, and He chose to show His redemptive powers. No matter what your sin, God always gives you a second chance, and a third, fourth, and fifth if necessary—whatever it takes for you to win.

Ruth is also mentioned in the lineage of Jesus (Matthew 1:5). She was a Moabitess; these were people with whom God was not pleased. In fact, God told them that because of their treatment of Israel, they could never enter His presence. The book of Ruth describes how this young Moabite woman married a Jewish man who fled with his family to her land because of a famine. Her husband died, her father-in-law died, and her brother-in-law died. Her mother-in-law, Naomi, decided to go back to her homeland and told Ruth to do the same—but Ruth clung to her and insisted on going with her.

Israel was a foreign land to Ruth with a God she did not grow up serving, yet she insisted on sticking with Naomi: "Ruth said, Intreat me not to leave thee, or to return from following after thee: for whither thou goest, I will go; and where thou lodgest, I will lodge: thy people shall be my people, and thy God my God" (Ruth 1:16). God gave her a second chance. She remarried in the land of her mother-in-law a wealthy man named Boaz. And she became the grandmother of King David and part of the lineage of Jesus.

There are so many other individuals throughout the Bible to whom God gave a second chance—Peter, Mary Magdalene, and many others. Do you see the pattern? As we close out this day, I want you to remember three things to help position yourself for your "take three," "take four," or whatever you need.

1. Forgive yourself. You have seen that God forgives you, so you have to take the position that if God believes you are forgiven and cleansed and if He remembers your sin no more, then you owe it to yourself to do the same.

2. Forgive others. When others have done you wrong, you have to move on. If you continue to rehearse what people have done to you and hang on to that hurt, then the comfort of the Holy Ghost cannot work in your heart (Acts 9:31) and you'll never get back on path.

3. Sin no more. There's no sense starting the pattern all over again. You want to move on to victory, don't you?

Control Yourself

Walk in the Spirit, and ye shall not fulfil the lust of the flesh.

—GALATIANS 5:16

IN STEP TWO OF our twenty-eight-day challenge, we are studying how to go through the valley, with the emphasis on "go through." You're not parking in the valley, and you're not derailed by detours you encounter along the way. You're keeping your eyes on your Shepherd, and you know He'll give you another chance if you mess up.

Today we're going to study how you act in the valley, because that will determine if you get to the mountaintop. Notice I didn't say how bad the problem is. I didn't say how hard Satan is attacking you. I didn't say whether or not God will show up. You know God is going to show up. The question is, Will you be in position to receive from Him when He does? How you operate in the valley will determine whether or not you get through it to the place where you are lifting your hands in victory with a gold medal around your neck because you have won.

Here is the key I want to give you today that will open a life of victory for you: *Control yourself.* We've already studied the life of Paul, who went from being the Osama bin Laden of his day because he was relentless in persecuting and killing believers, to one of the greatest apostles ever. Yet this man wrote these words about the battle that raged inside him:

> For we know that the law is spiritual: but I am carnal, sold under sin. For that which I do I allow not: for what I would, that do I not; but what I hate, that do I. ... For I delight in the law of God after the inward man: But I see another law in my members, warring against

thc law of my mind, and bringing me into captivity to the law of sin which is in my members. O wretched man that I am! who shall deliver me from the body of this death?

—ROMANS 7:14–15, 22–24

The word *carnal* means "flesh ruled." You are not a body, and you are not a soul. You are a spirit. You possess a soul, which is your mind, your will, and your emotions. And you live in a body. Your body is just your house. That's why you can't just fall in love with someone's "house." You better find out who is living in that house.

The Bible teaches that your flesh still has a sin nature. As a Christian, when you are faced with a temptation, you always have a choice. You can side with your spirit and do what God says, or you can yield to your flesh and do what your flesh wants to do. This is the battle Paul wrote about. Can you relate to it? He said he does the very thing he knows he shouldn't do—the very thing he hates doing. And what he knows he should do, he doesn't do: "For the flesh lusteth against the Spirit, and the Spirit against the flesh: and these are contrary the one to the other: so that ye cannot do the things that ye would" (Galatians 5:17).

Will you let the Devil do what he wants to do in this situation? Or will you let God do what He needs to do?

I always think of those old cartoons where Donald Duck was faced with a decision. The angelic Donald Duck would sit on one shoulder and the demonic Donald Duck on the other. One would say, "No, you shouldn't do that." And other would counter, "Yes, you should." Of course, Donald Duck always picked the wrong side or there wouldn't be a story.

What Is at Stake

The battle, of course, is much more serious than a Saturday morning cartoon. The battle is for your eternal salvation. We've studied how God gives us second chances when we mess up, but it's one thing to make a mistake and say, "Father I repent," and move on. It's another thing to keep living in that sin.

Now, here's where I might rattle your cage. This is a no-excuse zone. Today, it is time to look in the mirror and make some decisions. The outcome of this battle has nothing to do with Satan at all. Really, the outcome doesn't have a whole lot to do with God, either, because He has already done everything He is going to do. The outcome of this battle is based on whether you are going to line up with God or with the Devil. Will you let the Devil do what he wants to do in this situation? Or will you let God do what He needs to do? It is time to stop sleeping around with folks you are not married to. It is time to stop eating things you know you are not supposed to eat. It is time to stop overeating and going to the local buffet to pour poison into your body. It is time to stop cussing folks every time you get upset. It is time to stop smoking that cigarette as soon as you leave church. It is time to stop treating your wife like she is a slave or your husband like he is a little boy. It is time to stop watching things online you know you shouldn't be watching. It is time to stop looking at trash magazines in the grocery store checkout lines and then taking that trash home. It is time to overcome these things. And the one who decides the outcome is not Satan. It is not God. It is you. It may be the fight of your life, but God requires you to defeat it. He requires you to operate in self-control.

You may say, "I don't want to hear this. I want to do what I want to do." You certainly can do whatever you want to do. God will not force you to do anything. He didn't force you to get saved. He won't force you to live right. Just understand that the seeds you are sowing now will have a harvest someday. Every action has a reaction. You are in a war, and you have to acknowledge that or you will be taken right out. There is no such thing as, "I can't help myself." That excuse doesn't exist. What exists is, "I don't *want* to stop. I *want* to do this." There is no such thing as, "I can't help myself." Yes, you can. And God expects you to.

Today Is the Day

We are on day eleven of our challenge. If you really want to win in life and be victorious, it is time for you to declare war on your sin. Paul tells you how to be victorious in this battle:

> There is therefore now no condemnation to them which are in Christ Jesus, who walk not after the flesh, but after the Spirit. For the law of the Spirit of life in Christ Jesus hath made me free from the law of sin and death. For what the law could not do, in that it was weak through the flesh, God sending his own Son in the likeness of sinful flesh, and for sin, condemned sin in the flesh: That the righteousness of the law might be fulfilled in us, who walk not after the flesh, but after the Spirit. For they that are after the flesh do mind the things of the flesh; but they that are after the Spirit the things of the Spirit.
>
> —ROMANS 8:1–5

Paul boiled it down to one sentence: "Walk in the Spirit, and ye shall not fulfil the lust of the flesh" (Galatians 5:16). That's the bottom line. The war will continue to go on, but if you will be led by the Spirit every day, you won't fulfill the lust of the flesh.

One of the fruits of the Holy Spirit is temperance, or what we would call self-control (Galatians 5:23). So if you need more self-control, ask the Holy Ghost for it. Do this, and you will never side with your flesh.

Will you commit to do these four specific things?

1. I will look in the mirror and see if there are any areas in my life where my flesh is winning.

2. I will pray an hour every day.

3. I will be filled with the Word of God about whatever area I face. I will study what the Word says about it, memorize those Scriptures, and meditate on them.

4. I will say no to my flesh. I will make the right decision. When the Spirit of God shows me something, I know I still have a choice, and I will make the right one.

I'm not going to promise you that fighting this battle will be easy, but you'll be surprised what you're capable of. Just as athletes train their flesh, you can train your flesh to know the difference between good and evil and to make the right decision so that it won't always be this difficult. Make a decision to win by winning the war within.

What Are You Eating?

"A good man out of the good treasure of his heart bringeth forth good things: and an evil man out of the evil treasure of his heart bringeth forth evil things."

—MATTHEW 12:35

YESTERDAY WE ESTABLISHED THAT we need to operate in self-control. Today I want to go a little deeper to show you specific ways to operate in self-control—which will help you win the war within and get through the valley to the mountaintop.

"The word is sown; but when they have heard, Satan cometh immediately, and taketh away the word that was sown in their hearts" (Mark 4:15). It's possible for you to have the Word of God sown in your heart, but if you're not doing the right things, Satan can come and steal it from you. What enables him to do this? "And the cares of this world, and the deceitfulness of riches, and the lusts of other things entering in, choke the word, and it becometh unfruitful" (v. 19). First are cares of this world—weights, distractions, temptations, and anxieties. Next are the deceitfulness of riches—notice that Jesus didn't say riches; He said the deceitfulness of riches. Money in itself is not bad or good; it's neutral. What you do with it is bad or good. Finally are lusts, which are longings for things, especially those that are forbidden; it could be the opposite sex, position, fame, and many other things.

If the Word is in your heart, how can cares, the deceitfulness of riches, and lust even get to the Word there? Notice where they lodge: in the heart. Jesus said, "A good man out of the good treasure of the heart bringeth forth good things: and an evil man out of the evil treasure bringeth forth evil things" (Matthew 12:35). So if you have evil actions, it's because you have been putting some evil treasure in your heart. Understand that whatever you allow to get in your heart, you will eventually do. This is different from something getting into your mind. Your mind plays a role in this, and we will talk about that in a moment, but whatever you allow to get into your heart, you will eventually do. That is how you find yourself in a position where you love God and honestly don't want to sin, yet you keep finding yourself sinning. You seemingly can't stop yourself. It's because of what's in your heart.

So my question to you today is, What have you been eating? I am not referring to natural food; I am talking about what else you are consuming day to day. What input are you receiving? Because whatever is going in is what is coming out:

> That which cometh out of the man, that defileth the man. For from within, out of the heart of men, proceed evil thoughts, adulteries, fornications, murders, thefts, covetousness, wickedness, deceit, lasciviousness, an evil eye, blasphemy, pride, foolishness: all these evil things come from within, and defile the man.
>
> —MARK 7:20–23

If you are pouring evil things into your heart, then even though you may love God and you may intend to do the right thing, you will still find yourself living in sin. You will still find that your spirit is not overcoming your flesh, but instead your flesh is overcoming your spirit.

When Ananias and Sapphira lied about how much they were giving, Paul asked, "Why hast thou conceived this thing in thine heart?" (Acts 5:4). Notice how Peter used the word *conceived*. If it was conceived, there was obviously some seed. What is in your heart is what's going to be in your life. It will determine your behavior, and your behavior will determine your future. It will determine whether you have victory over the difficulty you face or are taken out by it.

Three Gates

The Bible says, "Keep thy heart with all diligence" (Proverbs 4:23). Don't just protect your heart, but do it with all diligence. Notice that you have control over your heart; that's why we talk about self-control. Guarding your heart requires you to understand where the threats come from and then to diligently protect your heart from their entry.

There are three "gates" where evil can enter.

1. Your mind. "Make no provision for [indulging] the flesh [put a stop to thinking about the evil cravings of your physical nature] to [gratify its] desires (lusts)" (Romans 13:14, AMP). Instead, "Whatsoever things are true, whatsoever things are honest, whatsoever things are just, whatsoever things are pure, whatsoever things are lovely, whatsoever things are of good report; if there be any virtue, and if there be any praise, think on these things" (Philippians 4:8). Again, you have control: "Think on these things." It's up to you what you think about. It may not be easy at first to change your thinking, but remember that self-control is a fruit of the Holy Spirit. You *can* do it.

2. Your eyes. "I will set no wicked thing before mine eyes" (Psalm 101:3). Job said, "I dictated a covenant (an agreement) to my eyes; how then could I look [lustfully] upon a girl?" (Job 31:1, AMP). What you look at, you begin to think on. So as a man, if you keep looking at a woman in a certain way, it doesn't take long to go from eyes to mind to heart to action. That is why you have to be diligent.

Can I be real with you? There are some movies with certain actresses that I just can't watch. It doesn't matter if I want to see the movie. I already know I am not going to be able to sit in the movie theater and look at her for two hours. That wouldn't make any sense. Guarding my heart means guarding my eyes.

3. Your ears. The Bible commends the man who "stoppeth his ears from hearing of blood, and shutteth his eyes from seeing evil" (Isaiah 33:15). Whatever you hear, you will think on. If you hear it enough, it will take up residence in your mind, and you will be thinking about it constantly, and it won't be long before it has an impact on your heart.

The Progressive Nature of Sin

What are you allowing into your heart through your eyes, ears, and mind? What are you allowing to be deposited in your heart? This is what happens when you allow yourself to yield to your flesh:

> The works of the flesh are manifest, which are these; Adultery, fornication, uncleanness, lasciviousness, idolatry, witchcraft, hatred, variance, emulations, wrath, strife, seditions, heresies, envyings, murders, drunkenness, revellings, and such like: of the which I tell you before, as I have also told you in time past, that they which do such things shall not inherit the kingdom of God.
>
> —Galatians 5:19–21

The word *lasciviousness* means "looseness" and can be translated as "wantonness." *Wanton* means "hard to control, unruly, undisciplined." It means you no longer have restraint. You find yourself in a position where you have a hard time stopping yourself. When you say, "I can't put down the cigarette," you have entered into lasciviousness. It's what's going on when you say, "I can't stop taking a drink. I can't stop sleeping with people I'm not supposed to sleep with. I just can't seem to control my temper. I'm addicted. I can't stop watching porn online."

If you keep yielding to the flesh, particularly in the area where you struggle the most, you'll soon have a monster in front of you.

Lasciviousness is not a place you arrive overnight. Sin has a progressive nature. When you feed your flesh by looking at things you're not supposed to look at, listening to things you're not supposed to listen to, thinking on things you're not supposed to think on, and doing things you're not supposed to do, you're on the road to lasciviousness. You're actually making your flesh stronger and your spirit weaker. Remember, you have a battle going on inside you between your flesh and your spirit. Whichever one is stronger will win.

If you keep yielding to the flesh, particularly in the area where you struggle the most, you'll soon have a monster in front of you. You will love God and want to be free but will seem unable to defeat the problem. The good news is that you can still defeat it. The bad news is that now you have a real fight on your hands because sin has a progressive nature.

Here are the five stages of sin—and notice that they are progressive: (1) attention (Satan tries to get your attention with whatever temptation it is), (2) attraction (you want it), (3) affection (you like it), (4) attachment (you really don't want to do without it), and finally (5) addiction (you can't do without it). This is the progressive nature of sin.

So if feeding your flesh feeds sin, how do you starve your flesh? Psalm 119:11 says, "Thy word have I hid in mine heart, that I might not sin against thee." How do you hide God's Word in your heart? Through those same three gates—your mind, your eyes, and your ears. So read the Word, study the Word, listen to the Word, and think about the Word. Change your diet. Instead of being consumed by this world, get consumed by God and His Word.

Back on day one, you made a list of areas in your life where you need victory. Go back to that list now and look at each one. Ask the Holy Spirit to show you if you have been feeding your flesh in some of these areas, and if so, how you can starve your flesh and feed your spirit. This may not apply to each situation on your list, but pray and ask the Holy Spirit to show you.

Stay in the Fight

Fight the good fight of faith.

—1 TIMOTHY 6:12

I WANT TO WARN YOU about something that may be happening to you. You've gone through nearly half of our challenge so far. You agree with what you're reading. You're *amen*-ing it. As soon as you turn the last page, however, the Enemy is going to start lying to you again. Just because you learned this information and have even begun to apply it, do you think the Enemy is going to step back and say, "Oh well, I lost that one. She's really strong now. I'll just go on to someone else"? Of course not. He's mad! You've got the victory, which means he's defeated—but because he never learns his lesson, he's going to try to recapture that ground he lost and take you out of the fight. He will always try, but he does not have to succeed. So I want to make sure you stay in the fight. I want to prepare you to live a life of victory so that you are no longer listening to the Enemy's lies but rather to the truth of God.

Yesterday we answered the question, What are you eating? We read Psalm 119:11, which says, "Thy word have I hid in mine heart, that I might not sin against thee." We studied the importance of hiding God's Word in your heart and how this will help you not sin. That is such a powerful spiritual principle that I want to revisit it today because it will help you stay in the fight.

The Five Attributes of Sin

When Satan comes calling, especially to someone who is spiritually strong, he doesn't announce himself. He comes in the back door and tries to lure you. Let's review the five attributes—or stages—of sin: (1) attention (Satan tries to get your attention with whatever temptation it is), (2) attraction (you want it), (3) affection (you like it), (4) attachment (you really don't want to do without it), and finally (5) addiction (you can't do without it). You don't want to wait until he's at the fifth stage to start fighting. You want to be in the fight at the beginning.

If the Enemy is trying to feed your flesh, then you've got to starve your flesh. When I say your flesh, I don't mean your body. I'm talking about the sin nature in the flesh. You want it to be so weak that it is a whimper, and you want your spirit man to be so strong that it is easy for you to do right. You want your spirit man to be growing stronger and stronger every day, while your flesh is getting weaker and weaker. Some folks say, "It is just too hard to live for God. It is too much of a fight, day by day by day." Honestly, it's not really supposed to be that hard. If it is that hard for you, it is because of this issue. It is because you have some stuff going into you. You are trying to mix motor oils. Do you remember that commercial a few years ago about not mixing brand X oil with the good stuff? If you're adding some brand X oil to the Holy Ghost oil in you, that's a recipe for disaster. If you're having a difficult time resisting the Devil, you are probably putting some bad stuff in and some good stuff in—and you have a battle going on.

If you're having a difficult time resisting the Devil, you are probably putting some bad stuff in and some good stuff in.

If you will starve your flesh, you will see victory. That means there are certain things you know you cannot listen to, watch, or think on. If you refuse to yield to your flesh, you will feed your spirit. You will find yourself in a position that it is not all that difficult to operate in self-control, even when the pressure is on.

How do you do this? Again, Psalm 119:11 says, "Thy word have I hid in mine heart, that I might not sin against thee." Words are the most powerful thing in the universe, especially God's words. This earth was created by His words. The Bible says it is still being upheld by His words. You, including your spirit, were created by His words. In fact, the Bible says that you are born again through the incorruptible seed of His word. The Bible says His words are spirit and life. His words are able. His words are powerful. His words are creative. His words are cleansing. Jesus said to His disciples, "You are clean through the word that I spoke to you." He prayed to His Father, "Sanctify them through thy truth: thy word is truth" (John 17:17). That is powerful. Jesus actually prayed for His Father to set you apart and make you holy through the word.

Notice Psalm 119:11 does not say "Thy word I have heard" but "Thy word have I hid." There is a difference. The word *hid* means "to hoard or reserve." The word we use today is "to deposit." Why do you take your money and put it in a bank? Because money in the bank is more protected than money under your mattress. If somebody wanted to rob you, it would be far easier for them to go into your home and just take all the money in the world that you have. It is far more difficult for them to take that money from the bank. That is what this verse means. When you hide God's Word in your heart, you've hoarded it, reserved it, deposited it, and protected it.

There are more verses that show this spiritual principle. Proverbs 4:20–22 says, "My son, attend to my words; incline thine ear unto my sayings. Let them not depart from thine eyes; keep them in the midst of thine heart. For they are life unto those that find them, and health to all their flesh." Hebrews 2:1 says, "Therefore we ought to give the more earnest heed to the things which we have heard, lest at any time we should let them slip." In other words, you have to keep giving attention to the Word so that it doesn't get uprooted from your heart and all of a sudden you find your-self living in a way you don't want to live anymore. Make sure the Word is abiding in you.

Jesus said, "If ye abide in me, and my words abide in you, ye can ask for what ye will, and it shall be done unto you" (John 15:7). He also said, "If ye continue in my word, then are ye my disciples indeed; and ye shall know the truth, and the truth shall make you free" (John 8:31–32). What does the Word set you free from? It sets you free from sin. So if you want victory over sin, then hide God's Word in your heart.

How do you do that? You use the same entities that caused sin to get into your heart: eyes, ears, and thoughts. Remember, these are the gates we talked about earlier. The Bible says that you should keep God's Word in front of your eyes, that faith comes by hearing, and hearing by the Word of God. It says you should study the Word, read the Word, and meditate on the Word every day. You might say, "I don't have time to meditate on anything." Really? You must not think at all, then, because you meditate every day on something. You may be meditating on the cares of this world, but you are meditating on something. Why not meditate on the Word of God so that you are hiding it in your heart? Instead of being consumed by this world, get consumed by God and His Word.

I have had the privilege of going to many of Kenneth Copeland's Believers' Conventions, and they are packed morning to late at night with five messages every day. You go to the morning session and hear a speaker who blesses your life. The next speaker gets up without taking a break, and he's off preaching. You have just enough time for lunch, and then you come back for more. Someone starts off the afternoon, and there's another speaker as soon as he finishes. You come back that night for more. I don't mean they preach for fifteen minutes, either. We're talking ninety minutes of the Word.

The first time I went to a convention, I thought, "I can't do this. I'm just going to two sessions, and that is all I can handle a day." The first person was so good, and the next person got up to preach, and I'm thinking, "I'll listen to him a few minutes and then I'll leave." And then all of a sudden, I got hooked. After lunch I thought, "I am going to go get some sleep," but somebody says, "Come on, we need to go to the next session," so there I am again—and it's so good. My flesh is saying, "You need to get some rest," but my spirit is getting blessed and blessed. Pretty soon it's evening, and I'm back for more.

What happens in a convention like this is that you get so inundated with the Word that you forget about everything else. I've had this happen more than once. I come out of the convention, and I've forgotten about all my problems. I'm fired up. I'm not going to lie—I'm sleepy, but I'm fired up. My faith is strong. My joy is strong. My character is strong—all because I took some time to get in the Word of God.

I'm not saying you have to do that every week, but you do need to get in the Word every day and allow it to abide in you. Here's what will happen. Just like sin is progressive, spiritual growth is also progressive. You will get stronger and stronger and stronger. The Bible actually teaches that you can reach a place where your body is trained, and your body will tell you the difference between good and evil because instead of feeding your flesh, you have been feeding your spirit. And that's how you can stay in the fight and be victorious.

Day 14

It Will All Be Worth It

Let us not be weary in well doing: for in due season we shall reap, if we faint not.

—Galatians 6:9

As we reach the end of step two and the halfway point in our twenty-eight-day challenge, you may feel like you've been doing everything you can to wait for victory in certain areas of your life, yet you're not seeing any victory. In fact, you may be ready to give up. You might say, "I just can't take it anymore. I'm tired of this. I can't put up with this another second."

You're not alone. That's why Paul wrote, "Let us not be weary in well doing." Notice he says, "Let us." In other words, whether or not you become weary in well doing is entirely up to you. Becoming weary is a choice. You can choose to give up, or you can choose to believe the Word. And if you do believe the Word, God promises that you'll reap "in due season." That's one of my favorite phrases in the Bible because it means there is a due date on your blessing. There is a due date on your reward. There is a date marked on God's calendar where you and His promise are going to meet. On that date, in that due season, you will get the reward He promised you if you don't give up.

Today, we're going to look at seven areas where you need to keep persevering even though you are weary and feel like giving up.

1. Live holy. I probably lost a lot of readers just by using that four-letter word *holy.* But it's a master key to having a successful life and pleasing God.

> By faith Moses, when he was come to years, refused to be called the son of Pharaoh's daughter; choosing rather to suffer affliction with the people of God, than to enjoy the pleasures of sin for a season; esteeming the reproach of Christ greater riches than the treasures in Egypt: for he had respect unto the recompence of the reward.
>
> —HEBREWS 11:24–26

Moses made a choice to live holy and side with the people of God rather than the wealth of a pagan nation. The Enemy may be trying to get you to back away from the commitment you made before God, but if you will make a choice to live holy and keep doing it, it will all be worth it. "Who shall ascend into the hill of the LORD? or who shall stand in his holy place? He that hath clean hands, and a pure heart; who hath not lifted up his soul unto vanity, nor sworn deceitfully" (Psalm 24:3–4). That sounds like somewhere I want to be.

2. Keep putting up with difficult people. If I didn't lose you on the first one, I may lose you on this one. "Walk worthy of the vocation wherewith ye are called, with all lowliness and meekness, with longsuffering, forbearing one another in love" (Ephesians 4:1–2). I don't know about you, but *longsuffering* is one of my

You can choose to give up, or you can choose to believe the Word.

least favorite words in the Bible. It's bad enough that God talks about suffering, but now He is talking about *long* suffering. We may be able to put up with somebody and do some short suffering, but *long* suffering? Lord, I don't know about that. Yet that is what He requires.

Forbearing here literally means to "put up with." We all know some people that we simply have to put up with, and sometimes they're right in our own house, office, or home group. The Word says you can't be weary in putting up with them. In fact, you have to love them and do what's best for them—all those things in 1 Corinthians 13. If you do this, you can rest assured that God will reward you. It will all be worth it.

3. Keep serving God by serving others. "God is not unrighteous to forget your work and labour of love, which ye have shewed toward his name, in that ye have ministered to the saints, and do minister" (Hebrews 6:10). If you are serving the people of God, you are actually serving Him. God will reward your work. He will reward the pain you went through so that somebody else can be blessed. He won't forget it. He's going to reward it—here on Earth, and in heaven also. You'll have a harvest in both places.

"For bodily exercise profiteth little: but godliness is profitable unto all things, having promise of the life that now is, and of that which is to come" (1 Timothy 4:8). Don't let the Enemy tell you, "You've been serving for so many years and you still haven't seen a breakthrough. So that obviously doesn't work. Just give up." That is a lie from the Enemy. You simply haven't reached your due season yet. Resistance is always the fiercest at the point of breakthrough, so your due season is probably right around the corner. Don't stop serving the ones God tells you to serve. It will all be worth it.

4. Keep on living to give. Don't get weary in your giving, even in a time of recession or when the economy doesn't seem to be right. "There is that scattereth, and yet increaseth; and there is that withholdeth more than is meet, but it tendeth to poverty" (Proverbs 11:24). The word *scattereth* implies two things: sowing in multiple locations and sowing bountifully. That doesn't mean giving a cent here and a cent there. It means giving bountifully and abundantly. It means you are living to give.

"Let him labour, working with his hands the thing which is good, that he may have to give to him that needeth" (Ephesians 4:28). God promises to make you rich so that you can be generous. You'll always have all sufficiency in all things so that you can abound in giving (2 Corinthians 9:8, 11). You don't have to worry if God can do it. The blessing of the Lord maketh rich. It is not your job to make rich. Your job is to live to give, knowing that God will increase you. "The liberal soul shall be made fat: and he that watereth shall be watered also himself" (Proverbs 11:25). It will all be worth it.

5. Be diligent in your assignments. "I have fought a good fight, I have finished my course, I have kept the faith" (2 Timothy 4:7). Notice that Paul had a course. You have one, too. We all have different courses and assignments from God. You are here for a purpose. You've been wired to carry out a kingdom mission, and it is your job to finish your course, which means you are going to have to be diligent in it. It's like running a marathon. You can't sit down at mile ten and take a break. You have to keep on going and finish the race, no matter how thirsty you are, what the weather is like, or anything else. You've got to keep going and be in constant effort to accomplish your goal of finishing the race.

It's the same concerning the assignments God has given you. You have to be diligent in those assignments. This applies in so many areas: your family life, your spouse, raising your children, your career. You have God-given assignments in each of those areas, and you have to be diligent in finding out what they are—what God expects of you—and then be diligent to complete the task. You want to hear Him say, "Well done." It will all be worth it.

6. Keep having faith in God. Paul refers to the "good fight of faith" (1 Timothy 6:12). It's actually the fight to stay in faith. The bottom line is that once you have taken a position of faith when you choose to believe God in whatever area it is, the Enemy immediately goes on assignment to try to get you out of faith and into fear. He knows if he can get you out of faith, he can win. That's why the Bible says, "Cast not away therefore your confidence, which hath great recompence of reward" (Hebrews 10:35). Continue to get in the Word of God about whatever area the Enemy is attacking you, and continue to confess the Word of God about that area. Don't ever let up. Keep your faith strong. Keep God's Word in front of your eyes (Proverbs 4:21). That implies intensity. Be committed to keep it there. Every day, look at the Word of God in that area so that no matter what happens, you have faith in God. It will all be worth it.

7. Keep chasing Jesus. Genesis 5:24 says, "And Enoch walked with God." Enoch chose to be someone who walked with God. Notice he didn't just visit God. He didn't just show up and say, "Hey, what's up, God?"

on Sunday or Wednesday or just when things got tough. He walked with God. One translation says, "He was in habitual fellowship with God" (Genesis 5:22, AMP).

When things get tough and you don't see the result, you are tempted to take it out on God. That is one of the silliest things Christians do. Yet most of us have been guilty of it at some point or another, saying, "What I was praying for didn't happen, so I'm not even going to bother to spend time in prayer or the Word anymore." No. That's not how you should react. Keep chasing Jesus. Keep following Him. The real prize in your Christian walk is Him. David made some mistakes, but God still said at the end of his life, "That is a man after My heart." For all eternity, we will know him as King David because he kept chasing God. Even in the wilderness, he said, "My soul follows hard after thee" (Psalm 63:8).

It will all be worth it someday when you enter heaven and are welcomed by all those you love who went before you. You will walk the streets of gold and dance with Jesus, celebrating Him. And you will say, "It was all worth it!"

I Can Win

1. What did you read during this section that surprised you or challenged you?

_____

_____

_____

_____

_____

_____

2. How has your understanding changed about your ability to be victorious in the areas you listed on day one?

_____

_____

_____

_____

_____

_____

_____

3. What are some of the areas where you need more self-control?

_____

_____

_____

_____

_____

_____

_____

_____

4. Where did the Holy Spirit show you that you've been feeding your flesh?

_____

_____

_____

_____

_____

_____

_____

_____

5. List the verses that God has quickened to you during this section. Use them as declarations during the next week to remind yourself of God's promises that you can win and be victorious, no matter what you face.

_____

_____

_____

_____

_____

_____

_____

_____

_____

6. Update the victory pages you filled out on day one (and continue updating them throughout the twenty-eight-day challenge). In which areas are you beginning to see victory?

_____

_____

_____

_____

_____

_____

STEP 3:

FOLLOW THE PLAN

With This Ring

Look not every man on his own things, but every man also on the things of others.

—Philippians 2:4

YOU ARE NOW READY to begin the third step of learning how to be victorious in all areas of life. In the first step, you learned to look up at God, not down at your problems. Next, you learned that everyone experiences times in the valley of the shadow of death, but you learned how to go through that valley rather than park there. Now you are going to learn how to follow God's plan—how to apply God's Word about victory to some of the most important areas of your life. We can't, of course, cover every area of life in this section, but you will learn how to take these principles and apply them to any area where you need to see victory.

We're going to begin with the family. If you want to change your city, state, country, or world, it begins in your home. Today, you are going to learn the key to having the kind of family life that God wants you to have—and the one you want to have, too. Home is supposed to be your paradise. The rest of the world is crazy enough as it is. You have to go out your front door and deal with all kinds of stuff. You should be able to come home and find a God-ordered paradise. You should walk in and see someone who loves you and whom you love in return. You should see your kids enjoying life. That is God's plan.

We're going to begin by looking at how you can have a winning marriage. If you're single, don't skip today because there's something here for you, too. Either you'll be married someday or you'll have an opportunity to minister God's Word to someone who is. So please stick with me.

It comes down to one very simple principle. I'm not saying it's simple to do, but it's a simple, basic, foundational truth upon which everything else in marriage is based:

> But he that is married careth for the things that are of the world, how he may please his wife. There is difference also between a wife and a virgin. The unmarried woman careth for the things of the Lord, that she may be holy both in body and in spirit: but she that is married careth for the things of the world, how she may please her husband.
>
> —1 Corinthians 7:33–34

The word *careth* implies attention and focus. This Scripture verse says that man's attention and focus are on the matters of this world. Notice that Paul didn't say how he can get his wife to please him. Notice that it says *please,* not appease. In other words, the husband should not just do enough to have peace in the home. God wants the wife to be satisfied by her husband.

The number one problem in marriages today is selfishness—living like it is all about me instead of like it is all about we.

Similarly, Paul said the wife's focus and attention should be on pleasing her husband. Notice he didn't say she is focused on how she can get her husband to please her or how her husband isn't meeting her needs. He said that her focus and attention should be on how she may please her husband. So clearly it is the will of God that the husband be satisfied by his wife.

The number one problem in marriages today is selfishness—living like it is all about me instead of like it is all about we. A lot of times, couples focus on what they are not getting from their mate. She says, "I'm not doing what he wants until he does what I want." He says, "I'm not doing what she wants until she does what I want." And so the marriage gets worse and worse because they don't understand this very simple principle of satisfying their mate.

It *is* very simple: Your job as a mate is to satisfy your mate. If there is a problem in your marriage, you need to look in the mirror and ask yourself if you are satisfying your mate. As long as you are pointing at your mate as the cause of all your problems, you are not going to get anywhere. As long as you are focused on what your mate is or is not doing, you are not going to have the kind of marriage you want. That's why Paul wrote, "Look not every man on his own things, but every man also on the things of others" (Philippians 2:4).

You can't satisfy your mate's needs without knowing what they are, so let's spend a moment on that. Here are the five needs of a woman and the five needs of a man. Women need affection (non-sexual touch), conversation, honesty and openness, financial support, and family commitment. Men need sexual fulfillment, recreational companionship, an attractive spouse, domestic support, and admiration. Spouses need to actively see these in their mates. Just like it is not good enough for a husband to say, "I love my wife; I just never tell her," it is not good enough for a wife to say, "I admire my husband; I just never tell him."

One of the main purposes for marriage is so that a husband and wife would be sexually fulfilled:

> To avoid fornication, let every man have his own wife, and let every woman have her own husband. Let the husband render unto the wife due benevolence: and likewise also the wife unto the husband. The wife hath not power of her own body, but the husband: and likewise also the husband hath not power of his own body, but the wife. Defraud ye not one the other, except it be with consent for a time, that ye may give yourselves to fasting and prayer; and come together again, that Satan tempt you not for your incontinency.
>
> —1 Corinthians 7:2–5

Look at how many words in that passage have a legal context. We normally see words like *render, due benevolence, defraud,* and *consent* in contracts.

Why would God use legal terms? Because when you marry someone, you enter into a covenant with them. At the altar, you make a covenant with your spouse, saying, "I will take care of your needs all the days of your life"—and that includes sexual needs for the reasons Paul outlined. I know this isn't romantic, but it is in the Bible.

One minister said his church had a problem: Too many single people were having sex, and too many married people were not. That is a big problem. It's not right for one spouse to withhold sex from the other—either as punishment or for whatever reason. The Bible says that if a wife or husband holds back from their mate, they are actually putting their mate in the temptation zone. God doesn't want you to get to the place where you are tempted. He doesn't want you to enter into temptation, because once you get into temptation, you are very close to stepping right into sin.

In the Old Testament, a new husband was not even allowed to go to war or focus on any other business for a year after marriage. He was supposed to stay home and "cheer up his wife which he hath taken" (Deuteronomy 24:5). The phrase "cheer up" doesn't mean she was depressed, but that he should make her happy and brighten her life. What wife wouldn't want that? "Live joyfully with the wife whom thou lovest all the days of the life of thy vanity" (Ecclesiastes 9:9). Shouldn't your marriage be so filled with joy no matter how long you've been married that the world will look at you and say, "I want what they have"? If you operate your marriage the way God says you should, that's what you'll have.

Here are seven keys to marital bliss based on God's Word.

1. It starts with a man. Note that in the creation story, it began with the man. Of course, our wives have responsibilities, too, but my point is that God started the relationship with the man first. (See Genesis 2.)

2. You need to date your mate. "Isaac was sporting with Rebekah his wife" (Genesis 26:8). This sporting they did was clearly in public because the king saw them. The word *sporting* means "to laugh out loud, to play with each other, to hug, kiss, and caress." When you were dating, I guarantee you didn't let a week go by without going on a date. You shouldn't after you get married, either.

3. It is a marriage of two. "Therefore shall a man leave his father and his mother, and shall cleave unto his wife: and they shall be one flesh" (Genesis 2:24). This passage is not just talking about sex but also about the marriage relationship. There are many ways you can wrongly bring others into your marriage—the kids, in-laws, outside friends, outside interests, pornography, or even idle chatter about your spouse. Don't do it.

4. Respect the man and honor the woman. This goes back to the needs we have just studied—but it is much more than fulfilling needs. God's Word commands it (1 Peter 3:2, 7, AMP).

5. Talk about everything. "Can two walk together, except they be agreed?" (Amos 3:3). Marriage is about walking together. It is impossible to be agreed without talking about it. Maybe that means asking some questions to make sure you understood what you think you heard because men and women speak different languages.

6. Let God be the referee. In every sport, a referee is there to tell if a player went out of bounds or broke the rules. Sometimes you need a referee in your marriage, and the best one is God. When you disagree about something, see what His Word has to say. Pray. Then act on what He tells you.

7. Praise your mate. Read Song of Solomon and see how one spouse should talk about the other. We all need affirmation, so make sure you nourish your mate in this way. Build each other up, and you will have a wonderful marriage.

Day 16

You Are the Father!

Children are an heritage of the Lord.

—Psalm 127:3

YESTERDAY WE STUDIED HOW you can be a godly spouse to your mate so that you can have a winning marriage. Today we're going to talk about being a godly father so that your children can win in life. Mothers and singles, please don't stop reading. In this section of the book, it's valuable for everyone to see what God's Word has to say to each of us, so please keep reading. There's truth here for you, too.

A recent survey of thousands of parents found that most of them had a survival-based strategy rather than a goal-oriented strategy when it came to raising their children. That's exactly what you don't want. You don't want to just survive or maintain during your kids' growing-up years. You want to purposely make sure you raise children who will become adults who will truly serve God.

> Children are an heritage of the Lord: and the fruit of the womb is his reward. As arrows are in the hand of a mighty man; so are children of the youth. Happy is the man that hath his quiver full of them: they shall not be ashamed, but they shall speak with the enemies in the gate.
>
> —Psalm 127:3–5

Do you notice to whom these verses are addressed? They're addressed to the father. There are many verses in the Bible that give wisdom about how to raise children, and most of them are written to fathers. Of course, the

Bible demonstrates a fundamental, critical role for mothers, too, but it's very strategic that so many "how-to" verses are aimed at fathers—because fathers have a great responsibility in raising their children. That's why the title of today's study is "You Are the Father." If you are a father, one day you are going to stand before God and He is going to ask you about how you raised your children—or didn't.

That word *heritage* means "an inheritance." The New Living Translation says, "They are a gift from the LORD." The Message version says, "Don't you see that children are God's best gift, the fruit of the womb is generous legacy." Kids are not just a bother or a money drain. They are a gift and God's blessing to you, and you need to see them as God sees them.

What happens when you look at them this way and actually put in place a plan to raise them? God gives you a promise: "Train up a child in the way he should go: and when he is old, he will not depart from it" (Proverbs 22:6). The word *train* does not mean "visit"; it means "to mold and to point." That requires more time than just showing up. It implies taking the time that's necessary to get the desired result.

Again speaking to fathers, the Bible says, "Ye fathers, provoke not your children to wrath: but bring them up in the nurture and admonition of the Lord" (Ephesians 6:4). The Amplified Bible says, "Rear them [tenderly]." This is not talking about physical growth, because that will happen no matter what. This is about spiritual growth and maturity.

You'll notice that none of these verses say it's the job of the church to train up a child. The church is a help and a partner, but it's the parents' job—particularly the father's job—to train up the child. Home, not church, is where a child's faith is nurtured.

As a father, here is my plan for raising my children to love God and serve Him.

1. Live your faith. God said of Abraham, "For I know him, that he will command his children and his household after him, and they shall keep the way of the LORD, to do justice and judgment; that the LORD may bring upon Abraham that which he hath spoken of him" (Genesis 18:19). Wouldn't you love to hear God say that about you? Children do what they see you doing, so if you live your faith in everyday life, it will speak a lot louder than any words you speak to them.

2. Have a weekly faith talk with your kids. Sit down with your kids and take the time to teach them the Word of God yourself. That means you need to open up the Bible with them, read a Scripture, and tell them what it means. Make it fun. Make it enjoyable. They need to be taught God's Word, just like you need to be taught God's Word.

> Therefore shall ye lay up these my words in your heart and in your soul, and bind them for a sign upon your hand, that they may be as frontlets between your eyes. And ye shall teach them your children, speaking of them when thou sittest in thine house, and when thou walkest by the way, when thou liest down, and when thou risest up.
>
> —DEUTERONOMY 11:18–19

3. Be consistent with church attendance. Your church can be your most valuable partner as you raise up your children in the way they should go. They can help you help your children to become all that God made them to be. We've already covered that you cannot turn over that responsibility to the church, but the church can be there for you. This happens when you follow Hebrews 10:25: "Not forsaking the assembling of ourselves together, as the manner of some is; but exhorting one another: and so much the more, as ye see the day approaching."

Your goal should be for your children to have a boring testimony.

4. Protect your children from exposure to bad influence. Your goal should be for your children to have a boring testimony. We all love hearing a good testimony, but wouldn't you rather spare your children going through that heartache and misery? "Ye did run well; who did hinder you that ye should not obey the truth? This persuasion cometh not of him that calleth you. A little leaven leaveneth the whole lump" (Galatians 5:7–9). Don't let even a little bit of the wrong type of influence get into your children's lives. That requires constant vigilance on your part—school, friends, Internet, TV, movies, games, after-school activities, books, music, recreation, clothes, and every other area of their lives.

5. Provide consistent correction. "Foolishness is bound in the heart of a child; but the rod of correction will drive it far from him" (Proverbs 22:15). If you don't address the foolishness in the heart of your children, they will become fools—and the Bible says the fool has said in his heart that there is no God. If foolishness is bound, that means it doesn't go easily. You have to give consistent correction. The Bible even talks about the rod of correction. As a parent, you should require holiness, which means when you see things going on in the world around you, you must speak against those things so that your kids have a very clear view of what is right and what is wrong.

6. Develop godly habits. By the time your children leave home, they should have the daily habits of mature Christians. You teach your kids to brush their teeth, do their hair, and all the other things. You ought to teach them to pray and read their Bible every day, too. By the time they are teenagers, they ought to be getting up early and praying like you do. Of course, they can't do that if you are not doing it yourself.

7. Pray for your children. The Bible says that praying fervently for someone is like giving birth to their spiritual maturity (Galatians 4:19). I regularly pray over my children the prayers that Paul prayed in Ephesians 1 and 3, Colossians 1, and Philippians 1.

If you were to switch places with Jesus, how would He raise your children? How much time would He spend with them? How would He talk to them? Would He make sure they were taught the Bible? Would He monitor what they watch on TV? Train your kids like you are Jesus. In spite of the many negative influences around today that often make it difficult to raise children correctly, you can be that kind of father to them.

Single Parents: Raising Children Who Win

A father of the fatherless, and a judge of the widows, is God in his holy habitation.

—Psalm 68:5

ᴀ ʟɪᴛᴛʟᴇ ɢɪʀʟ ᴛᴏʟᴅ ʜᴇʀ father that she learned about Adam and Eve in Sunday school, so he decided to see how much she remembered. "Did you know Adam and Eve sinned?" he asked.

"Yup," she answered.

"What did God do to them as a punishment?"

"He made them have kids."

In spite of the ups and downs of raising children, children are a reward and a blessing. Today we focus on single parents, particularly single mothers, and God's special blessing and provision for them. If you're not a single parent, please don't skip today's study because I'm going to share spiritual truths that will be a blessing to you, too—plus you'll be better able to minister to single parents you know or meet.

God loves your children, and today we're going to see that if you let Him, He'll be a father to them. Let's begin with a story in Deuteronomy that has nothing to do with parenting but everything to do with how God operates (so therefore it affects parenting). The Moabite king, who hated Israel, hired the prophet Balaam to put a curse on Israel so that he could defeat them in battle. As we've already seen, a curse is the empowerment to fail, and a blessing is the empowerment to succeed or win. The Moabite king was hoping for a curse, but here's what he got: "Nevertheless the Lord thy God would not hearken unto Balaam; but the Lord thy God turned the curse into a blessing unto thee, because the Lord thy God loved thee" (Deuteronomy 23:5).

Satan hates the nation of Israel and tried to wipe them out. (He still does this.) But God had another plan. He not only thwarted the curse, but He turned it into a blessing. If Satan had just left them alone, they wouldn't have gotten this extra blessing. However, not only were they not harmed, but they were more blessed. God took a situation where Israel's enemy meant them to be cursed and defeated and instead made them blessed, prosperous, and successful.

However you became a single parent—whether it was because you had a child out of wedlock, somebody walked away, or somebody died—Satan may have meant it for evil, but God has plenty of experience turning what was meant to be evil into good. God will take what Satan meant as a curse on your life, and He will cause it to be a blessing on your life and the life of your kids.

So many people say that children growing up in single-parent homes are destined for trouble, and in the natural there may be an argument for that. But when you choose to serve God and follow His instructions, He will step in and make sure your children get back on track. He'll make sure they have success and experience the future He has for them. He'll take what could have been a test and turn it into a testimony. God always has a Plan B, and as long as you follow God's plan, your children's future will be great and wonderful.

When the Bible says that God is with you, that means that His blessing is on you. You're empowered to prosper.

Let's look at some examples of single parents in the Bible to see how God turned curses into blessings for them. Hagar was a single mother. God promised Abram and Sarai a child, but when it didn't happen according to their timetable, Sarai suggested that

Abram sleep with her maid, Hagar, and they would then raise the child as their own. (See Genesis 16.)

Hagar gave birth to a son, Ishmael. Later, when Sarai finally conceived and had her own son, Isaac, she convinced Abram to send Hagar and Ishmael away. Mother and child were in the desert, about to die of thirst and hunger, when God heard their cries: "God opened her eyes, and she saw a well of water; and she went, and filled the bottle with water, and gave the lad drink. And God was with the lad; and he grew" (Genesis 21:19–20).

Aren't you glad that God can take you from a place of being completely out of water to a place where suddenly you're standing in front of a well? When the Bible says that God is with you, that means that His blessing is on you. You're empowered to prosper.

In football, a coach can throw down a challenge flag to dispute any ruling by the referees, even one that results in a touchdown. The challenge flag means that the referees have to review the play, and often they overturn the original call. God is the one with the challenge flag. Maybe it looked like the enemy scored and that it was all over for you and your family, but God is the one who will step in and say, "Hold on. The ruling is overturned. You're not defeated. Your future is not aborted." Instead, God will put the ball back into your hands, and as you follow Him, He'll make the way for you to get in the end zone and say, "Look what God has done."

There are many other examples in the Bible of God providing for single parents: a poverty-stricken widow and her son (1 Kings 17); Esther, who was raised by her cousin (Esther 2:7); and Eli, who raised Samuel (1 Samuel 3). God always has a Plan B, and if He needs a Plan C, He's got a Plan C. If He needs a Plan D, He's got a Plan D. He loves your children, and He will be a father to them if you will let Him. He will defend them. Deuteronomy 10:18 says, "He doth execute the judgment of the fatherless and widow." Psalm 10:14 says, "Thou art the helper of the fatherless." Psalm 68:5 says, "A father of the fatherless, and a judge of the widows, is God in his holy habitation." Notice the word *is*. It doesn't say, "One day God *will* be a father of the fatherless." No, God—today—*is* a father to the fatherless. To those who don't have a living father or a father in the home,

God says, "I am their father." The Word says He loves, provides, protects, teaches, guides, gives mercy, defends, and avenges the fatherless. Is there a better father than the heavenly Father?

Seven Tips for Single Parents

Here are seven important ways that single parents can partner with God to raise godly children.

1. Be a godly example. This is especially true if your child is not in your home and may be living with an ungodly parent. You be the example of God in their lives. They'll see light in the midst of darkness. If you do it right, they'll do it right—and they'll be much more likely to listen to you.

2. Talk with your child. Even more importantly, let them talk to you. Cultivate an atmosphere where they feel comfortable talking to you— where, in fact, you're the one they come to first. How else can you give them godly direction and, when needed, correction if you don't know what's going on?

3. Don't allow them to blame themselves or God for both parents not being in the home. You have to tell them, "It wasn't your fault. No, God didn't do this to you. No, this was not God's plan for you—but God does have a plan for you."

4. Teach them to forgive. Frankly, the thing that will help your children the most is your ability to forgive. If you don't forgive, then you can forget about them forgiving. If you don't recognize that your heart is filled with bitterness toward your ex, that bitterness will eat you alive—and it will eat your children alive, as well. Teach them how to handle hurt, and model it yourself.

5. Avoid baby-mama or baby-daddy drama. You may still have to deal with a person you can't stand. Or your ex may marry someone else and now you have to deal with that person, too. This can be a recipe for disaster and drama. You can't control them, but with God's grace you can do what Romans 12:18 says: "If it be possible, as much as lieth in you, live peaceably with all men." They may consider themselves to be at war with you, but you have to intentionally live at peace with them.

6. Don't share your problems with your children. The Bible doesn't say to confess your faults to your kids. They're not your personal counseling center or your best friend. That doesn't mean you can't be a friend to them, but they're not your best friend; you're their parent. Your kids don't need to know everything that's going on in your life. Let your kids be kids.

7. Don't introduce them to people you're dating until you're going to get married. The courtship process is for testing—you're trying to find out if this person is Bozo or Boaz—so don't bring your children in on that. Wait until you know the relationship is of God, and then He will blend your family.

God loves your children, and if you let Him, He'll be a father to them. Despite what they are facing in life, they will win.

Matchmaker, Matchmaker

> Whoso findeth a wife findeth a good thing.
>
> —Proverbs 18:22

I

F YOU'RE SINGLE AND read through the past few days on subjects that seemed like they were for someone else, thank you—today is for you! And if you're not single, my counsel to you is the same as I gave to singles the past few days: Please don't skip today's reading. Just because you're not single doesn't mean God can't speak to you through the Scriptures and material offered here today. And learning today's lesson means you'll be able to minister to the singles God brings into your life.

Many single women have mentioned to me that there is a dearth of eligible godly men. They fret about statistics that say there's no hope for them to marry. Some men feel the same way about finding a wife. My answer to them is simple: "You only need one!" God has a person in mind for you, and if you'll follow His direction, you will enjoy being a part of a match made in heaven.

I want to give you five keys that will put you in a position where God can bring you the kind of person you want for a spouse. These keys will also help you have a marriage that wins. During the past few days, you've read about a lot of problems that families and married couples can face. I can't guarantee you'll avoid all of those problems, but you can avoid a lot of them—and a lot of pain and misery in the process—by following these five keys.

Key 1: It Starts With a Man

In Genesis, God makes man, forms him out of the dust of the ground, breathes life into him, and gives him the task of taking care of the garden. There are a number of things that this passage teaches about a real man. A real man is already in the garden. A real man knows who made him, and he follows Him. A real man realizes he is second and God is first. A real man has received Jesus. He is done trying to be God. A real man knows God's calling for His life. A real man is already living faith at home long before his future wife shows up. If he is sleeping around, he is still a boy. If he doesn't want to give a tithe, then he is not ready. If there is a whole bunch of drama going on in his life, he needs a little bit more time.

A real man is doing his best to obey God. A real man will not try to sleep with you before marriage. A real man will keep his word. A real man will never lift his hand to hit a female. That is a coward. Go hit another male and see what happens. A real man has a job, just like Adam had a job. A real man can provide for his wife and family according to 1 Timothy 5:8. A real man has a dream in his heart and is bold enough to chase it. He knows where he's going and what God has called him to do. God told Adam to tend to the garden, name the animals, and more. If a man doesn't know what he was born to do, you don't want to hook up with him. You need to know where you are going together before you marry him.

Key 2: The Man Is the Hunter; the Woman Is the Hunted

Judges 21 tells a story about men from the tribe of Benjamin looking for wives among a group of young women who were dancing and praising God. The men were the hunters, while the women were the hunted. Today it's the exact opposite. A single man comes into church, and all he is trying to do is praise God, but there are single women all around trying to get his attention. We've got this backward. The Bible says, "He that findeth a wife findeth a good thing" (Proverbs 18:22). Men are supposed to be the ones pursuing women, not the other way around.

I was on a panel for a well-known secular magazine and a question about this came up. The majority of women in the room believed it was fine for them to approach a man. You know what that made me feel like? Like I was in a room with desperate women. I don't say that to be mean, but I was seriously thinking, "Is it that bad that they feel like they have to approach a man instead of being honored by a man approaching them?" No. Let the man be a hunter and the woman be the hunted.

A real man knows who made him, and he follows Him. A real man realizes he is second and God is first.

Sometimes single men think they need a "thus saith the Lord" word from God before they even approach a single woman. Once you have your life in order, you don't need to hear God say, "She's the one," before you even speak to her. If you're attracted to her, talk to her. God will show you what you need to know as you go through the process of dating, but that process doesn't start if you never even approach her.

Key 3: Let God Be the Matchmaker

In Genesis 24, Abraham sends his servant to get a wife for his son, Isaac. I am so glad it doesn't work like this today. I love my parents, but I didn't want them to pick my wife. I could hear my dad saying, "Son, she's anointed." And I would say, "But, Dad, she's ugly." No, I'm just kidding, but that's how things were done in Isaac's day.

Look at what Abraham told his servant: "He [God] shall send his angel before thee, and thou shalt take a wife" (v. 7). Did I just read about a matchmaking angel? Did the Scripture just show me that heaven itself would get involved in bringing a man and a woman together? A few verses later, the servant himself prays for God's direction in this search. God did get involved, and He brought Rebekah to Isaac. He will do the same for you if you will trust Him: "In all your ways acknowledge him, and he shall direct thy paths" (Proverbs 3:6). This applies not just to the "meeting" stage but the "getting to know you" stage as well. During the first month of the dating process, you should be trying to learn as much about the person as you can. God is your matchmaker, so you need to be praying throughout the entire process.

Key 4: Hands Off

We're talking about no sexual sin here. You can't have any wardrobe malfunctions, and you have to date in public. You can't be cuddled up on a couch with the person you are trying to date, even if another person is in the room. We're talking about two grown people, and if they are Christians, they have been trying to live holy, which means their bodies are rebelling. It doesn't make any sense to put yourself in dangerous situations, being all cuddled up against each other. You can love God, speak in tongues, know the Word, and quote half the Bible, but you can still mess up if you put yourself in dangerous situations. If you don't mess up now, you are going to be extremely frustrated, and you'll just mess up later. That's why it's critical to date in public. If you are dating someone who has a problem with that, it's a good sign to end the relationship immediately because it's not going where you want it to go.

Key 5: Take Your Time

If you're single, this is probably the last thing you want to read, but it's true. There's no hurry. The Bible says to prove all things. What does that mean? Put it to the test. Is this good or is this bad? Is it God or is it me? You can't do that in three months. At my church, we require that couples date for a year before we will marry them because it takes at least that long to get to know a person. My wife and I dated for almost two and a half years before we got married—and we still learned a lot of things about each other after we got married. Marriage is an eye-opener, and you want to go into it with your eyes open as much as possible. Know what you are getting into.

During the dating process, listen to your support system, whether it is your family, your godly friends, or your church family. The Bible says that in the multitude of counselors, there is safety. Don't listen to those who say your biological clock is ticking. Let God be your matchmaker. "Delight thyself also in the LORD: and he shall give thee the desires of thine heart" (Psalm 37:4).

Heaven's Health Care

Beloved, I wish above all things that thou mayest prosper and be in
health, even as thy soul prospereth.

—3 JOHN 1:2

T HAT IS A POWERFUL Scripture and proves that God's will is for you
to be in good health—yet the world is suffering from an epidemic
of sickness and disease. In fact, to find someone who does not
have some type of medical condition in their body is rare. In the US,
there has been an ongoing debate about health care because we are
looking for ways to combat this problem more effectively.

The term *health care* means "the field concerned with the maintenance or the restoration of the health of the body or mind." It is also
defined as any of the procedures or methods in this field. The title of our
study today is "Heaven's Health Care" because heaven is concerned with
the maintenance and restoration of the health of your body and mind. If
you have received Jesus as your Lord and Savior, you are already enrolled
in heaven's health-care system. He pays the premium for you every month.
(He prepaid it two thousand years ago.) You are automatically enrolled,
and you have access to the benefits any time you need them. In fact,
healing is an emergency procedure because heaven's health-care system has
provided for you to walk in health all the days of your life.

I don't know about you, but I am glad to be a part of heaven's health
care. No longer do I have to worry if my doctor is covered. My doctor's
name is Jesus, and He covers me. I don't have to worry if my medicine is
covered. I get my medicine from the Word of God. It doesn't cost me a

thing. I don't have to worry about my job dropping my insurance or raising the copay. I am in the body of Christ, and I am staying here all the days of my life. My insurance is not going anywhere. Healing belongs to me, and I am walking in health all the days of my life.

Is that what you want? My goal today is to help you to enjoy the benefits of your heavenly health-care policy, to help you receive your healing, and if you are already walking in your healing, to help you continue to walk in health.

Let's look at a key scripture to set the foundation for this: "Who his own self bare our sins in his own body on the tree, that we, being dead to sins, should live unto righteousness: by whose stripes ye were healed" (1 Peter 2:24). This is, of course, talking about Jesus. He bore your sins in His body on the tree, and the Bible teaches that at the same time that He bore your

If you have received Jesus as your Lord and Savior, you are already enrolled in heaven's health-care system. He pays the premium for you every month.

sins, He bore your sickness: "But he was wounded for our transgressions, he was bruised for our iniquities: the chastisement of our peace was upon him; and with his stripes we are healed" (Isaiah 53:5). He bore your sins and your sicknesses. In fact, we know that sin is the root cause of sickness. Sometimes when I read 1 Peter 2:24, I read it this way: "Who his own self bare our sicknesses in his own body on the tree, that we, being dead to sickness, should live unto health: by whose stripes ye were healed."

Every bit of that is accurate, and we will prove that. There is evidence that the price for your sins has been paid—the stripes on His back are proof that He bore the punishment of your sins and that He took your place. Since He took your place, you don't have to bear sickness; you are completely free from it. The Bible says, "By whose stripes ye were healed"— not that you're going to be, not that you're hoping to be, but that you already were healed. It happened at the moment He took the stripes. You can look back and say, "That is the moment where He took the stripes, and that is the moment I was healed."

When you were born again, you were born into this world, spiritually speaking, and you were born healed. It's like a newborn baby is born into the world. In fact, while I was working on this chapter, my cousin had a baby. That baby was born healthy—and that happened to you spiritually when you said, "Jesus, come into my life." You became a brand-new creature. You became a babe in Christ. You were born healed, not with sickle cell, cancer, asthma, or anything else. You were born healed. Why? Because Jesus paid the price for your sickness almost two thousand years ago. At that moment, in the eyes of God, you were healed. At that moment, healing belonged to you simply because you received Jesus as Lord of your life, "by whose stripes ye were healed."

Some people argue, "That Scripture is talking about your spirit being healed." But there is no scripture in the Bible that says salvation is just your spirit being healed. The Bible says that when you made Jesus Lord of your life, you became a new creature. You became somebody entirely new on the inside. Your spirit didn't get patched up; your spirit was replaced. So this is talking about your physical body, and the word *healed* here means "cured or made whole." At that moment two thousand years ago, you were cured of whatever sickness was in your body. At that moment two thousand years ago, you were made whole of whatever problems were in your body. However your body was broken was taken care of. You are whole today.

I want you to see that you need to accept God's Word as truth instead of what you see or what you feel or what somebody else says. I don't care what the doctor says. I don't care what my body says. I don't care what you think you see in my body. I say that before God and man, I am healed because of what God's Word says. Why would God's Word say, "I wish above all things that thou mayest . . . be in health," if that were not His will?

Accessing Your Policy

There is one very specific principle that I want you to see that will give you access to this. You already have the policy; you just need to know how to access it—and that's what we're going to cover today.

"My son, attend to my words; incline thine ear unto my sayings. Let them not depart from thine eyes; keep them in the midst of thine heart. For they are life unto those that find them, and health to all their flesh" (Proverbs 4:20–22). Isn't that amazing? This verse says that God's Word is actually medicine that brings health to your body. One of the words in the definition of *life* is "strength." So God's Word gives strength—and it doesn't just give strength to your spirit man, but it also gives strength to your physical body. The word *health* here means "curative or medicine." So God's words are medicine to all the flesh—every part of you, physically and emotionally.

There is such power in God's Word. He said, "Be," and creation was created. If He created your body with His Word, He can heal your body with His Word. The psalmist wrote about individuals who were sick because of their sin, but God "sent his word, and healed them" (Psalm 107:20). When the sick and oppressed came to Jesus, in some cases He didn't even lay hands on them. He didn't spend three hours in prayer over them. He just spoke His word over them and they were healed. God's Word heals.

Sometimes we get into trouble when we are talking about healing because we look to a man or we look to a method. God may use a man or a method, but He expects all of us to grow up to a place spiritually where we don't need a person or a method to receive our healing. All you need is to open up the Word of God and let His words heal because He said they are medicine for all your flesh. If you have something wrong with your lungs or your liver, you take a pill and it knows right where to go to bring healing. When you get God's Word in you, it actually gets in your spirit and unlocks the anointing of God into your body—only it doesn't just mask symptoms like medicine does; it actually eliminates sickness. It doesn't just deal with the pain; it deals with the cause. One word from God will heal your body. If you don't believe that, look at Abraham. God said, "So shall your seed be," and he and Sarah were healed of barrenness.

All it takes for you to receive a manifestation of your healing is to get enough of God's Word on the subject abiding in you. Do you realize that? Put that Word inside your heart so that out of the abundance of the heart, the mouth will speak and the sickness will be gone. We should get to the point where we're putting away our glasses because we don't need them.

I don't know what is in your body or what came from your family line, but today let's declare war on every form of sickness or disease. Open up your policy that proves you're enrolled in heaven's health-care system, and put it to work for you.

Day 20

Take Your Medicine

My son, attend to my words; incline thine ear unto my sayings. Let them not depart from thine eyes; keep them in the midst of thine heart. For they are life unto those that find them, and health to all their flesh.

—PROVERBS 4:20–22

A FEW YEARS AGO, I was preaching a series about healing at our church in Georgia. After one of the services a woman sent this testimony:

> I was sitting in service and was challenged with some sinus issues. I had a pain in my sinus cavity down the left side of my neck. As Pastor Butler was preaching the message tonight, the left sinus cavity began to clear up. Before he called to lay hands on anybody who needed healing, my sinus cavity was completely clear, healed forever.

Nobody laid hands on her. Nobody cast sickness out of her. All we did is what we are doing now—preaching the Word. She was healed right in her seat because God's Word heals.

If you study Jesus' ministry, He went from place to place, preaching, teaching, and healing. We often try to switch that around so that it's healing and a little preaching and teaching, but that's not the pattern Jesus used nor the one we should follow. Remember when He went to His hometown and they wouldn't let Him preach? There were no healings there. We want to be healed, but we don't want to hear. We want the results of the medicine without taking the medicine, but that's not how it works.

Imagine if you went to your doctor and he prescribed some medicine for you. You went to the pharmacy to fill it and then you put the bottle on the counter in your kitchen—but you never actually opened it and took the medicine. It doesn't do your body any good just to have that bottle sitting on the counter. You have to open it and take the pills according to the number and frequency that your doctor prescribed. In the same way, it doesn't do your body any good simply to know that God's Word heals you. You actually have to follow God's prescription: "My son, attend to my words; incline thine ear unto my sayings. Let them not depart from thine eyes; keep them in the midst of thine heart. For they are life unto those that find them, and health to all their flesh" (Proverbs 4:20–22).

Notice all the commands in this prescription: attend, incline, let them not depart, keep them, find them. Those are all commands about the Word of God.

Notice all the commands in this prescription: attend, incline, let them not depart, keep them, find them. Those are all commands about the Word of God. The Word will heal you, but you have to get it abiding in your heart first. And that's what we're going to talk about today. How do you do that? God's prescription for your healing is actually a four-step process outlined in these verses from Proverbs. You may do one or two, but God's prescription is for you to do all four.

Step 1: "Attend to My Words" (v. 20)

The word *attend* means "to prick up your ears, to hearken." We would say "to pay attention." Make this a priority that has your main attention. Notice that He says to attend to His words versus your feelings, versus what other people may say, or versus what your body may say. Don't pay attention to any of those things, but pay attention to God's Word about healing. What does His Word say? Focus on that. Put God's Word first. What ought to get your undivided attention is God's Word on healing because God's Word heals.

You may have to shift your schedule around so that you can do this, but what is your priority? If you want to be healed, you know what your answer should be. I am a big sports fan, and the Lord has had to deal with me more than once about reading the sports page before reading the Bible or giving it more time and attention than I do the Word of God. God may deal with you about some things that are out of place in your life, too. He has no problem with you enjoying life, but it begins with enjoying Him. He is the number-one thing that you are supposed to enjoy. All the other things are just added perks and benefits that He created for you to enjoy.

Step 2: "Incline Thine Ear Unto My Sayings" (v. 20)

You need a constant, careful, diligent, reverent, and prayerful study of God's Word on healing. You're not just hearing the Word when you come to church on Sunday morning or Wednesday night. All week long, every day, you're searching the Word. You're reading books. You're listening to teachings. You're positioning your ears to hear God's Word and direction for you. Remember, the verbs in this scripture verse are not laid-back verbs; they're commands with intensity. You've got to press your way into them.

Step 3: "Let Them Not Depart From Thine Eyes" (v. 21)

God's Word will not get into your heart without going first through your ears or your eyes. So there is intensity involved in this statement, too. The more intense your sickness, the more intense you should be about following this step. The word *intensity* means "the amount of energy being transmitted." You'll have to expend a lot of energy actively pursuing God's Word. Don't let His Word *not* be in front of your eyes. The symptoms in your body will always be reminding you and lying to you, saying you are sick. So you need to make sure you have His Word in front of your eyes to counter those lying symptoms. If you keep the Word on this subject in front of your eyes, eventually you will see yourself in the Word. You will see yourself well. You won't see yourself having to check your sugar every day. You will see yourself forgetting what it is like to have diabetes. You won't see yourself having to get radiation treatment. You will see yourself completely healed and preaching and testifying to others.

Step 4: "Keep Them in the Midst of Thine Heart" (v. 21)

We have already studied the parable of the sower from Mark 4. The Enemy always tries to steal the seed, and he can do that if it's not planted in good soil. That's why it's critical for you to plant the Word in your heart and then keep it there. The thing about life is that the seed is always getting uprooted. Whatever word you are putting inside you, life is always trying to uproot it. The Enemy is always sending things your way to uproot it, so you have to keep it down. It's similar to a beach ball in a swimming pool; you have to keep pushing it down or it pops up. That's how you have to keep the Word down in your heart. Again, it's purposeful, intense activity on your part.

Proverbs 4 says that God's Word will be medicine to all your flesh, so if you are not in a position where that has happened yet, it is probably because you are missing a step or you just need to continue with the step until the Word is abiding in you to a place where healing takes place. Here are five practical ways you can do this so that you are continually taking God's medicine—His Word: (1) Read and think on it every day; (2) read from an anointed book or devotional on divine healing every day; (3) confess healing over your body every day; (4) listen to teaching on healing every day; and (5) praise God that you are healed every day—not *going to be* but that you *are* healed.

When I went to Rhema Bible Training Center, we used to sing a song that said, "It is so good to be healed. It is so good to be healed. By His stripes, I know I am healed." We'd have a conference, and you'd see people who couldn't even walk, but they were singing, "It's so good to be healed." Those were the very people who ended up shouting by the end of the conference because God healed them.

Remember, you have access to heaven's health-care system. You have access to God's medicine, and you have unlimited refills of His prescription. Consistency and intensity to follow His plan are the keys to your breakthrough. How long will you put this off? How long will you suffer when you don't have to? How long will you pay the amount of money you are paying for medicine and doctor's visits when you don't have to? I am not interested in settling for less than what Jesus paid for. How about you?

Day 21

Be the Boss—Part 1

The curse of the LORD is in the house of the wicked: but he blesseth the habitation of the just.

—PROVERBS 3:33

IN STEP THREE OF our study, we're learning how to apply God's solutions to every area of your life so that you can be victorious. One of the areas where nearly every Christian needs victory is in the area of finances. In fact, it's such a problem that we're going to devote two days to studying how God wants you to win financially and how you can release that victory. The world around you may be in a recession, but you don't have to allow recession into your home. The recession does not have to impact your financial life. You don't have to just hang on, hoping the economy will turn around. No matter where you are in your financial life, God can take you from financial ruin to financial prosperity if you will use your faith and authority in Him.

Over the next two days, we're going to look at seven steps to help you do this. In our church, we have seven steps leading from the sanctuary to the platform. When I've preached this message in my church, I've used those steps to show that you can't just leap from one level to another; there are specific steps you have to take. For you to get to the place where you're truly kicking the recession out of your home, there are specific steps you must take, too.

Step 1: Restore Your Faith in God

There are hundreds of verses throughout Scripture about finances—including promises that His desire is to bless you so that you can be a blessing. I wrote about these in my book *Not in My House*. (If you haven't completed that twenty-eight-day challenge yet, I encourage you to do so.) God's Word is very clear about finances, so when you do not believe and say what He is saying about your financial situation, you miss the first step to financial prosperity in your life. And of course you can't proceed to step two until you do step one. Everything in the kingdom of God is by faith.

Step 2: Repent for Where You Missed It

Proverbs 27:23 says, "Be thou diligent to know the state of thy flocks, and look well to thy herds." You probably don't have any flocks or herds today, so how do you translate that to life in the twenty-first century? It means you have to know the state of your finances and then apply God's principles to that area. You have to obey the scriptures about finances just as much as any other scripture. If you refuse to tithe or give offerings, if you don't have a budget, if you don't follow your budget, if you live above your means, if you don't know what is coming

If you look at what you have as seed, then you have a truckload of harvest in your future.

in and what is going out, you're not doing what it takes to be financially healthy. You aren't being "diligent" to know the state of your "herds."

That's why recession has gotten into the house of many of the just. They left the door open, and the Enemy took advantage and brought ruin into their lives. If that describes you, you must repent of where you missed it. That means more than just saying, "God, I'm sorry I got in this mess, and I know I did things wrong that brought me here." It means you have to go in the opposite direction and do what it takes to be financially healthy.

Step 3: Reinvest in the Kingdom System

As a believer, you operate on a different system than the world. Your system is based on seed time and harvest. It doesn't matter what is going on in the world around you. If you sow seed, you get a harvest. If you don't sow seed, you don't get a harvest. I hear people say, "I'm claiming a hundredfold"—but if they're not sowing any seed, a hundredfold times zero equals zero. You have to sow something to reap something; that's kingdom economics.

The widow in 1 Kings 17 was so poor that she was about to prepare her last meal for herself and her son, and then they planned to die. The man of God came and said, "Give me some water. Give me a little cake." She replied that this was hardly enough for a last meal—and she became afraid. The problem was that she looked at what she had as harvest. He looked at what she had as seed. She said, "This is all I have." He said, "This is all you need."

As long as you look at what you have as harvest, that is all you are going to have, but if you look at what you have as seed, then you have a truckload of harvest in your future. If you want to kick recession out of your house, you have to reinvest in the kingdom system. If you don't, you're actually creating an environment in your home where recession can come in.

Step 4: Race to Your Place

Jesus asked His apostles a question to remind them of what happened when He sent them out: "When I sent you without purse, and scrip, and shoes, lacked ye any thing?" (Luke 22:35). When Jesus asks a question, He's not looking for information. He already knows the answer. He was reminding them of how He had provided for all their needs—money, shoes, everything—because they were where He *sent* them. There is a difference between being sent and going. If God sends you on an assignment, He will supply all your needs to get there, while you are there, and to get home again.

When Jesus asked what the disciples lacked when He sent them, all of them replied "Nothing." So that tells me when they walked into a city to preach the Gospel and they had no money, no food, and no clothes, God made sure money came to them. God made sure food was placed before them, shoes were put on their feet, and they were well taken care of while they were carrying out His assignment. That is the key phrase: "while they were carrying His assignment." When they were doing what He sent them to do versus what they decided to go and do, the provision was there.

A lot of Christians are not winning financially because they are too busy chasing the American dream rather than being in their God-ordained place and fulfilling their God-given assignment. Just because you have a nice check coming in doesn't mean you are in God's assigned place. Many have learned that the check can go away real fast, and you better have God on your side when it does.

It is time to find out where God wants you and then race to that place. I say "race" to it rather than "go" to it because time is short. We are in dangerous times. Many people have already been taken out during these times. You need to race to get in your place right now. If you don't know where that place is, ask God. He won't hide it from you.

Tomorrow, we'll look at three more steps to help you be victorious financially.

Be the Boss—Part 2

And God is able to make all grace abound toward you; that ye, always having all sufficiency in all things, may abound to every good work.

—2 Corinthians 9:8

YOU'RE ABOUT TO BEGIN the last week of this challenge, and I hope you're beginning to see victory in the areas you listed on day one. Today, we're continuing our look at how to be victorious in our finances. Yesterday, we looked at the first four steps to help you get to the place where you've kicked recession out of your house. Let's look at three more.

Step 5: Receive Heaven's Instruction

God told Elijah to prophesy to wicked King Ahab that there would be a terrible famine throughout the land (1 Kings 17:1), and the famine came just as God warned. It was so bad that there wasn't even any dew. That's dry.

Yet God gave Elijah very specific instructions on how He would provide for him in the midst of the coming famine. First He told Elijah to go to a certain brook, where he could drink water. (Remember, He'd already said there would be a drought with no dew.) Then He promised to send ravens to bring food to Elijah every morning and evening. Next He told Elijah about a specific woman in a specific village whom He had already commanded to feed the prophet. And it all came to pass exactly as God said it would.

I want you to notice that the Word of the Lord that came to Elijah was entirely about provision. It was all about making sure the man was provided for. Some people think that talking about money and provision is not very spiritual, but the topic is all over the Bible. If it is in the Bible, it is spiritual.

You might say, "But God sent him to a brook and the brook eventually dried up. I thought he was where God told him to be." He was, but sometimes natural circumstances will impact what God can use to get the provision to you. That doesn't change the fact that God is going to get it to you. God just had to change channels. Instead of using the brook and some ravens, next He used a widow in a village called Zarephath.

Notice that when Elijah ran out of water, God didn't just immediately give him water. He gave him a word. God doesn't always directly meet your need. Many times, He gives instruction, and as you obey the instruction, the blessings follow your obedience. That is what happened here. It required a measure of faith. We see the same principle at the Cana wedding feast. Jesus told the servants to fill jars with water. They had to obey first—and then the water turned to wine.

You might pray, "God, I need this amount of money for this purpose. God, where is my harvest for that? God, can You come through in this area?" You are looking for cash, but God wants to give you a word. If you just obey that word, then you will have the cash. You will have the increase, but you have to obey that word. The instruction you obey is the future you create. No obedience means no provision, but obedience means provision. So receive heaven's instruction, and then act on it.

Step 6: Reclaim Your Wealth God's Way

When I was little, we'd go into a store, pick out something, and sometimes my mother would put it on layaway. The store would hold on to it until we finished paying for it, and then we could come and get it. In the same way, the wealth of the sinner is laid up for you. It is on layaway. There are verses throughout the Bible that show this:

> A good man leaveth an inheritance to his children's children: and *the wealth of the sinner is laid up for the just.*
>
> —PROVERBS 13:22, EMPHASIS ADDED

If you received Jesus as Lord of your life and you are living that way, you are part of the just, so the wealth of the wicked is stored up for you.

> He that by usury and unjust gain increaseth his substance, *he shall gather it for him that will pity the poor.*
>
> —PROVERBS 28:8, EMPHASIS ADDED

> For God giveth to a man that is good in his sight wisdom, and knowledge, and joy: but to the sinner he giveth travail, to gather and to heap up, *that he may give to him that is good before God.*
>
> —ECCLESIASTES 2:26, EMPHASIS ADDED

> This is the portion of a wicked man with God....Though he heap up silver as the dust, and prepare raiment as the clay; *he may prepare it, but the just shall put it on, and the innocent shall divide the silver.*
>
> —JOB 27:13, 16–17, EMPHASIS ADDED

You may say, "I need a New Testament scripture on that." I've got it for you. Who was one of the people ministering with Jesus? "Joanna the wife of Chuza Herod's steward…who ministered unto him of their substance" (Luke 8:3). Herod was not the just, nor was Joanna's husband, Chuza, or he would have been following Jesus. So Herod would pay Chuza, and he would give money to Joanna, who would in turn help finance Jesus' ministry. The wealth of the sinner was coming into the hands of the just so that the Gospel could be preached.

You may be asking a very logical question: "If the wealth of the wicked is stored up for the just, why isn't it in my hands?" The answer is because you have to claim it. You have to go back to the layaway window with your ticket of faith and claim your harvest by praying for it or calling it into your life (Mark 11:24). Then receive it in Jesus' name.

There are three ways that God gets wealth out of the hands of the wicked and into the hands of the just: unexpected income, instructions from God (such as when Jesus told Peter he would find a fish with a coin in its mouth), and our jobs. So go and claim it—and read why in the next step.*

Step 7: Return to Your Purpose

Please remember this important principle: God is transferring wealth from the wicked to you not to make you wealthy for your own sake; it is so that you can help reach the lost. Why does God want to get money into your life? Is it just so that you can meet your needs? Is it just so that you can have your desires—the house you want, the car you want, the clothes you want? We know the Bible teaches us that God wants us to enjoy life. Is there a higher purpose than that? Can your money impact somebody else's eternity?

God is transferring wealth from the wicked to you not to make you wealthy for your own sake; it is so that you can help reach the lost.

> Every man according as he purposeth in his heart, so let him give; not grudgingly, or of necessity: for God loveth a cheerful giver. And God is able to make all grace abound toward you; that ye, always having all sufficiency in all things, may abound to every good work.
>
> —2 Corinthians 9:7–8

God wants to get money *to* you so that He can get it *through* you. It is like breathing. You have to inhale in order to exhale. God wants you to inhale it and exhale it. Get it to give it. If all you do is inhale and you never exhale, you've got a problem. If that is how you are in life, you are the wicked rich man. You are the one who is storing up wealth for someone

---

* For more teaching on this, see my mini-book *Wealth of the Sinner, Harvest of the Just.*

else—for the just man, for the person who understands the real purpose is, "I get it to give it."

If you want to recession-proof your home and your family, I encourage you to follow all seven of these steps. Remember, they are steps, not tips. You can't skip one and double up on another. If you diligently follow all seven, you will be positioned to help people instead of being the one always needing help. That is really the will of God.

Day 23

Victory Over Pornography and Other Addictions

But among you there must not even be a hint of sexual immorality.

—Ephesians 5:3, NIV

ODAY WE'RE GOING TO talk about some heavy issues that need to be discussed in a godly, spiritual setting: how to experience victory from pornography and other addictions. If you don't struggle with pornography, please keep reading. You'll learn principles that will set you free from whatever addictions you may encounter in your own life, and you'll learn how to help others experience victory, too.

God's standard is that there should be no hint of sexual immorality in our lives, yet we live in a world where temptation and sexual sin are rampant. Things that are clearly wrong before God are accepted as normal. In fact, people will criticize you for not doing things the wrong way. Consequently, many men—many Christian men—have more than a hint of sexual immorality in their lives: lusting after women they are not married to, looking at pornography, or being involved in masturbation.

Sexual sin not only costs you, but it costs your wife, too, if you are married. It costs your kids, because just like righteousness can be passed down, so can generational sin. Do you recognize this pattern? Grandma had a child out of wedlock. Her daughter had a child out of wedlock. Her daughter had a child of wedlock. When a man or woman lives a lifestyle consumed in sexual sin, it gets passed on to their kids.

Pornography and sexual immorality are pervasive problems in the church, and we can't act like they're not. Instead of soldiers who can help God save the world, He's got men who are still stuck in the infirmary. Every week, they come to church just so they can make it through the next week. That is not God's destiny or plan for them or you. This is an issue that many battle, and we need to deal with it right now.

I have good news for you. Jesus has already dealt with it so you can experience victory in this area. Look at these scripture verses:

> Then said Jesus to those Jews which believed on him, If ye continue in my word, then are ye my disciples indeed; and ye shall know the truth, and the truth shall make you free.... If the Son therefore shall make you free, ye shall be free indeed.
>
> —JOHN 8:31–32, 36

> Forasmuch then as the children are partakers of flesh and blood, he also himself likewise took part of the same; that through death he might destroy him that had the power of death, that is, the devil; and deliver them who through fear of death were all their lifetime subject to bondage.
>
> —HEBREWS 2:14–15

> Therefore we are buried with him by baptism into death: that like as Christ was raised up from the dead by the glory of the Father, even so we also should walk in newness of life.... Knowing this, that our old man is crucified with him, that the body of sin might be destroyed, that henceforth we should not serve sin. For he that is dead is freed from sin.... For sin shall not have dominion over you: for ye are not under the law, but under grace.... But now being made free from sin, and become servants to God, ye have your fruit unto holiness, and the end everlasting life.
>
> —ROMANS 6:4, 6–7, 14, 22

You just read ten verses showing that if you have received Jesus, you are free from sin. Your old man has died; when he did, the sin nature died in you. You were freed from sin. That means you don't ever have to sin another day in your life. That means if you happen to be bound in sin right now and the Enemy is saying you will never get free of it, what he is telling you is a lie. Jesus has already set you free. Jesus has already given you everything you need to walk in victory in this area.

Here are five facts about sexual sin that will help you understand where we are going today:

1. Sexual sin is simply a series of bad choices evolving into bad habits.

2. Sexual sin is a habit. It is not genetic. You weren't born this way.

3. Sexual sin works like a habit.

4. Sexual sin is a habit, but it fights like an addiction.

5. You can bring bad habits and hormones under the control of your spirit.

The good thing about sexual sin being a habit is that if it lives like a habit, it can die like a habit. Here are a few things you can do to help you fully enjoy freedom. Remember, these principles will free you from any addiction—smoking, illicit drugs, alcoholism, or any other type of addiction.

1. Make a Quality Decision to Change

Romans 12:2 says, "Be not be conformed to this world: but be ye transformed by the renewing of your mind." In other words, God is telling you to choose to change. Your habit is costing you—and most likely everyone connected to you—big time. God, your mate if you're married (or your future mate if you're not), your children, your extended family, your job, your church, and you all suffer as a result of your decision to continue with this destructive habit. Make a quality decision today that you are done with it and that you will work with God so your decision becomes a reality.

2. Come Closer to God

Jesus said to pray so that you would not enter into temptation (Matthew 26:41). I have found that the more quality time I spend with God in His Word, in prayer, and in church, the less tempted I am to sin. Make a concerted effort to "draw nigh to God" more than you ever have before. As you do, He will help you to be completely free, as He has helped so many others before you.

3. Develop the Right Habits

We've established that all addictions at their core are just habits. The good thing about that is that you can replace a bad habit with a good habit. There are some good habits that you need to develop that will help you win over this addiction.

Cast down tempting thoughts. Every sin starts with thought. This is true of addictive behavior, as well. This battle must be won in your mind. And 2 Corinthians 10:3–6 shows how you are to deal with thoughts that don't line up with God's Word. When thoughts of that addiction come into your mind, open your mouth and speak God's Word over your life. You can't fight thoughts with thoughts, so you have to open your mouth and speak the Word. A good scripture is John 8:36, so declare, "Jesus has made me free from _____ [name the addiction], and I'm free indeed." Philippians 4:8 is another great scripture that you can use as a sword to fight off the Enemy's attack against you.

You can't fight thoughts with thoughts, so you have to open your mouth and speak the Word.

I must give you a warning here, though. You have developed a habit of thinking in this way, so you may have to cast down these thoughts and speak the Word about it hundreds of times in the first few days. But keep doing so, and you'll enjoy the freedom Jesus bought for you. That's what happened with Jesus in Luke 4. When Satan tempted Him, Jesus responded with the Word of God, and eventually Satan departed from Him for a season.

Speak the Word of God over yourself. You may ask, "Didn't you just say that?" My answer is, "Yes! But this is worth repeating!" The Bible says that your entire body is controlled by your tongue (James 3:3–5). Even if you find yourself about to smoke a cigarette (or whatever your habit has been), when you light it, between each drag speak, "God loves me. I don't need this. Jesus has made me free, and I'm free indeed!" You may feel a bit strange doing this, but after a while it will break through to your spirit, and you'll be totally free.

Make a covenant with your eyes. Job said, "I dictated a covenant (an agreement) to my eyes; how then could I look [lustfully] upon a girl?" (Job 31:1, AMP). The Message translation says it this way: "I made a solemn pact with myself to never undress a girl with my eyes." Men, you have to make a covenant with your eyes—and there's no better time than this very moment. Say, "I make a decision that from this day forward that I am not undressing a woman with my eyes. From now on, I am not looking at the apple. From now on, I have made a decision that I am going to live honorably before God in this way."

Bounce your eyes. You can't always control what you see. It may be on a billboard when you're driving down the highway or an ad in the middle of a football game. You can't control what comes in front of your eyes, but you can control what you do with your eyes once you see it. Treat it like you just touched a hot stove. If you put your hand on a hot burner, you'd pull it back very quickly. That means look away. Change the channel— *zap!*—and come back in thirty seconds. (That's a good reason for men to hold on to the remote.) I call that "bouncing your eyes," and you can develop a habit of doing this. Your flesh will get weaker and weaker and your spirit stronger and stronger.

And ladies, you need to do the same thing. There are images all around you that you don't need to be looking at, either. You need to develop the habit of bouncing your eyes, too. For men and women, Jesus felt that your purity was worth dying for, so you ought to feel that it is worth fighting for. "I will set no wicked thing before mine eyes: I hate the work of them that turn aside; it shall not cleave to me" (Psalm 101:3).

4. Remove Yourself From Temptation

The Bible says to abstain from the appearance of evil (1 Thessalonians 5:22) and to remove yourself from evil (Proverbs 4:27). Jesus said, "Watch and pray, that ye enter not into temptation" (Matthew 26:41). A popular saying today is, "If you can't stand the heat, get out of the kitchen!"

Whatever your habit is, do not allow yourself to be in a position to be tempted to do it. That means if you're an alcoholic, avoid the bars or liquor stores. If illicit drugs are your problem, then avoid the places where you know you can get them. If porn is your problem, get those X-rated channels out of your house (and off the Internet). If you have friends who engage in this behavior, cut them off. Jesus said, "If your eye offends, you pluck it out" (Matthew 5:29). In other words, do whatever it takes to stay free from this sin. You may have to take some drastic measures to make sure you don't enter into temptation and, ultimately, commit this sin.

I encourage you to connect with a good Bible-believing church and seek counseling there. The Bible teaches that two are better than one and that a brother is born for adversity. If there's any time we need each other, it is when we are in trouble, so allow those whom God has called to serve you in this capacity to help set you free at last.

I Can Win

1. What did you read during this section that surprised you or challenged you?

_____

_____

_____

_____

_____

_____

2. Pick one of the specific areas covered in this section—marriage, children, health, finances, etc. How has your understanding changed about your ability to be victorious in that area?

_____

_____

_____

_____

_____

_____

_____

3. Quote two Scriptures, one from the Old Testament and one from the New Testament, that show God's solutions to that specific area.

_____

_____

_____

_____

_____

_____

_____

4. What action steps has the Holy Ghost spoken to you about taking regarding the specific area you mentioned above?

_____

_____

_____

_____

_____

_____

_____

5. List the verses that God has quickened to you during this section. Use them as declarations during the next week to remind yourself of God's promises that you can win and be victorious, no matter what you face.

_____

_____

_____

_____

_____

_____

_____

_____

6. Update the victory pages you filled out on day one (and continue updating them throughout the twenty-eight-day challenge). In which areas are you beginning to see victory?

_____

_____

_____

_____

_____

STEP 4:

DO YOUR VICTORY DANCE

Day 24

Dream Again

"Hath he spoken, and shall he not make it good?"

—Numbers 23:19

A s we begin our fourth step, you may be wondering why it's called "Do Your Victory Dance," when perhaps you haven't yet experienced victory. That's because you need to get to the place where you dance in faith *before* you have the victory in order to actually *get* the victory. Football players do a victory dance in the end zone, but I'm asking you to do your victory dance before you get into the end zone—because that is the kind of faith that will help you get in the end zone. Do you follow? When Joshua and the people were marching around the walls of Jericho, they danced and shouted before the walls came down, and that helped them experience victory. Do your victory dance before you get in the end zone.

You have a lot to shout and dance about because you are about to step into the ultimate opportunity zone. God is going to do some great things for you. He is going to give you the breakthroughs you have been waiting for and praying for, and the suddenlies you have been believing for. This is going to be the best season you have ever had in your life. You may read these words and struggle to accept them and believe them because, frankly, you've dreamed big in the past and somewhere along the way your dreams got derailed. So my assignment today is to help you dream again, to get you to a place where you are like that five-year-old little boy or girl who believed anything was possible—and then to help you dance in victory about it.

While I was working on this book, the city of Detroit where I live had reason to celebrate because our beloved Detroit Lions football team was in the playoffs. It had been twelve long years since that had happened—a long, difficult time to be a Lions fan. We stuck with them and believed in them, though, even during seasons when it seemed nothing would ever change.

You may feel the same way. It may feel like more than a dozen years that you've been believing God for your dream to happen. And you may have given up on your dream. Today, I want to restore that dream to you, and I'm going to start by reminding you of God's character.

"God is not a man, that he should lie; neither the son of man, that he should repent: hath he said, and shall he not do it? or hath he spoken, and shall he not make it good?" (Numbers 23:19). One of the things you must do is stop judging God based on what man can do. To lie, of course, is to deceive. God doesn't say A when He really means B. He doesn't try to trick you into believing in A when He knows that B is what He is really going to bring about. No. God does not lie. We see that again in Hebrews 6:18 and Titus 1:2. It is impossible for God to lie. Numbers 23:19 says He will "make it good." That's His character. That's who He is. He is the one person you can count on 100 percent. If He said it, He will do it. He will do whatever it takes to make it good.

God wants you to dream again. And you can do that because you can count on Him. I didn't say the government. I didn't say someone you love or a friend you can trust. I am talking about God. "For I am the LORD: I will speak, and the word that I shall speak shall come to pass" (Ezekiel 12:25). This is the God you can trust to bring about your dreams.

> For as the rain cometh down, and the snow from heaven, and returneth not thither, but watereth the earth, and maketh it bring forth and bud, that it may give seed to the sower, and bread to the eater: so shall my word be that goeth forth out of my mouth: it shall not return unto me void, but it shall accomplish that which I please, and it shall prosper in the thing whereto I sent it.
>
> —ISAIAH 55:10–11

God might have spoken something to you that you haven't yet experienced, but it shall come to pass. It shall not return to Him void. That is the character of God.

Remember, our goal today is to get you dreaming again. Let's look at someone in the Bible who gave up on his dream years ago—in fact, you can measure it in decades. When Abram was ninety-nine years old, God appeared to him and reminded him of the promise He had made decades earlier—to make him the father of nations:

> And when Abram was ninety years old and nine, the LORD appeared to Abram, and said unto him, I am the Almighty God; walk before me, and be thou perfect. And I will make my covenant between me and thee, and will multiply thee exceedingly. And Abram fell on his face.
>
> —GENESIS 17:1–3

By this time, Abram does have a son, but through Hagar, not Sarai. Sarai is still barren. So Abram is thinking that God is going to do all these things through Ishmael, the son he had with Hagar. Abram can accept that because it's doable. Yet God throws a wrench into Abram's nice version of what is about to happen. God tells him he will have a child with Sarai and that she will be a mother of many nations. Abram's reaction is to fall on his face and laugh! The man started off falling on his face in reverence, and now he falls on his face mocking God. I think it is safe to say that he didn't believe what God was saying. He had lost the dream of having a son with Sarai. He had it at one time back in Genesis 12, but he was younger back then. And Sarai was, too.

When did the dream die? It was already dead when Abram agreed to Sarai's plan to take Hagar, and Ishmael was born. But God came back and said, "No. I am still doing it through you and Sarah." Abram had a son named Isaac, whose name means "laughter." So Abram went from laughing at God to laughing with God.

What happened here? Clearly, God did a few things. First, He changed Abram's name to Abraham, which means "father of many nations." He changed Sarai's name to Sarah, which means "mother of many nations." So every time they said each other's names, they were agreeing with God's Word. God was building their faith. Every morning, when Abraham woke up and saw the sand, he saw the promise of God—that his descendants would be more plentiful than the sand. Every night, when he saw the stars, he saw the promise of God—that his descendants would be more numerous than the stars in the sky. In Romans 4, Paul writes about what happened to Abraham. He went from being someone who had lost his dream to being able to dream again. He broke through the temptation to not believe God.

There are so many other examples of individuals throughout the Bible who lost their dreams but regained them. Imagine David, who was called to be king when he was just a child. He fought giants, bears, and lions, and he eventually ran for his life from the hands of the reigning king who was so jealous that he tried to kill him—repeatedly. When you read some of the melancholy psalms, I personally believe David had given up on his dream, yet somewhere he got hold of it again, and of course he did become king.

Read the Word and remind yourself what God did for others. Make a list of what He did for you. Add to it every day.

How about you? Have you let go of your dream? Have you given up because you've waited years, even decades? Here are four keys that will help you dream again.

1. Constantly Remind Yourself of the Faithfulness of God

Notice I use the word *constantly*. You may need to do this daily, even hourly. Abraham, "being fully persuaded that, what he had promised, he was able also to perform" (Romans 4:21). Read the Word and remind yourself what God did for others. Make a list of what He did for you. Add to it every day. Constantly remind yourself that you are leaning on the arm of God, not on the arm of flesh.

2. Ignore Your Circumstances

"And being not weak in faith, he considered not his own body now dead" (v. 19). When Kenneth Hagin was fighting sickness, he told the Lord that he was trying to "consider not" the pain, and God told him to consider Him. Consider not what you see with your earthly eyes. Consider Him. Set your eyes on God, not on the circumstances. That is not easy to do at times, but you can make a choice and ask God for His grace to do it.

3. Praise God Because It Is Done

Notice I didn't say "because it *will* be done" but "because it *is* done." Abraham "staggered not at the promise of God through unbelief; but was strong in faith, giving glory to God" (v. 20). Unbelief will make you stagger. Belief will make you praise. Praise God because it's already done. Praise is the opposite of staggering. This is where your victory dance comes in.

4. Confess It Like It Is Done

"[God] calleth those things that be not as though they were" (v. 17). That's what happened with Abraham. God called it. It hadn't happened yet, but God talked about it like it had. And Abraham got to the place that he talked about it like it had happened, too. You've got to call your mountain moved. You've got to call your blessing received. You don't wait until it happens to say, "I got it." Faith says, "I have it," before you have it. Faith says, "It is done," before you see it done. Confess it like it is done.

Dream again. Then do your victory dance.

Day 25

Flashback

I will remember the works of the LORD.

—PSALM 77:11

HAVE YOU EVER FELT like the psalmist who penned these words: "I am so troubled that I cannot speak.... Will the Lord cast off for ever? and will he be favourable no more? Is his mercy clean gone for ever? doth his promise fail for evermore? Hath God forgotten to be gracious? hath he in anger shut up his tender mercies?" (Psalm 77:4, 7–9).

Have you ever felt like that? Have you been in such a dire situation that you didn't see any way out? If you're like the rest of us, you can answer that question with a resounding "yes." How you respond to times like these helps ensure your ultimate victory. Look how the psalmist responded: "I will remember the works of the LORD: surely I will remember thy wonders of old. I will meditate also of all thy work, and talk of thy doings" (vv. 11–12). That was his remedy that helped him to be encouraged and continue to believe God: He remembered what God did for him in the past. In fact, he meditated on it and talked about it. The word *remember* means "to make a mark."

Suddenly the psalmist's entire countenance changes. By verses 13–14, he says, "Who is so great a God as our God? Thou art the God that doest wonders." Is this the same guy? What a turnaround! And it happened because he made a decision to remember what God did for him. I call this a "flashback." When you stay in faith is when you get the victory. When you are going through difficult times, do what the psalmist did: Remind yourself of God's faithfulness. Remember all those times when God showed up for you and made a way out of no way. Recall when He showed there is nothing impossible to Him. You need to have a flashback to all those times. Reminding yourself of these things will encourage you and strengthen your faith and will help you to get the victory that you and God want you to have.

Did you know you have the ability to do this—to flashback? You control what you think about. The word *remembrance* in one way or another is used five times in Psalm 77. And one of those times, the psalmist says, "I call to remembrance." In other words, "I am reaching out in my mind and I am bringing this memory back to the forefront."

You can probably remember what your last meal was. You can remember details about your graduation from high school or things about your first boyfriend or first girlfriend (and you may wish you didn't remember them!). The point is that

When you are going through difficult times, do what the psalmist did: Remind yourself of God's faithfulness.

you can determine what you think on. Sometimes you need to turn the channel in your mind to remind yourself of the times when God came through for you.

Remember the Promises God Has Kept in Your Life

Remembering is not just some kind of feel-good activity. It's a powerful way to ignite your faith. In fact, God commands you to remember. The word *remember* is found 146 times in the Bible. The word *remembrance* is used fifty-two times. Many of the feasts the Lord commanded Israel to celebrate involved remembering what He had done for them at specific times. In Genesis, God called Jacob to go to Bethel. Jacob said, "I will make there an altar unto God, who answered me in the day of my distress, and was with me in the way which I went" (Genesis 35:3). This was a flashback for Jacob of all the times when God came through for him and protected him and made him wealthy. During the Lord's Supper, Jesus said, "This do in remembrance of me." He expects you to remember.

Remember When God Met Your Needs

The disciples saw Jesus multiply bread and feed thousands of hungry people, yet a few moments later they had forgotten the miracle and were worried He was angry because they didn't bring food for the journey. Look at Jesus' response: "Which when Jesus perceived, he said unto them, O ye of little faith, why reason ye among yourselves, because ye have brought no bread. Do ye not yet understand, neither remember the five loaves of the five thousand, and how many baskets ye took up?" (Matthew 16:8–9). Jesus reminded them that He not only met their needs, but He gave an overflow.

Remember the Victories You've Already Won

One of the greatest examples of the power of remembering is David. The teenage boy stood before King Saul and boldly proclaimed that he would fight the giant Goliath—and win. When Saul questioned his bravado, David told him about all the times he had been tending sheep in his father's fields and killed lions and bears with his bare hands. He was giving the king a flashback—remembering what God had already done for him in the past to prove what God would do for him in the present.

Remember What It Was Like to Live Without Him

Just spend a few moments remembering what life was like before you met Jesus and committed your life to Him. Remember that Jesus loved you enough to pay the ultimate price to get you out of hell. Surely He'll do what it takes to get you out of whatever trouble you're in now.

You may be facing your own Goliath—and if so, you need to have a flashback. I am here to remind you of the lion that God helped you defeat in your past, of the bear that God helped you defeat in your past, of the Goliath that God help you defeat in your past. I am here to remind you that God has given you victory before and that God will give you victory now.

I love where the Word of God says, "Now thanks be unto God, which always causeth us to triumph in Christ" (2 Corinthians 2:14). It doesn't say that He always watches you triumph. It says He gets involved. He *causes* you to triumph. Have a flashback, and remind yourself of what God has already done for you. Then do your victory dance.

Day 26

Yes, He Can!

Now unto him that is able to do exceeding abundantly above all that we ask or think, according to the power that worketh in us.

—Ephesians 3:20

I USED TO LOVE THE TV program called *24*. It was about a twenty-four-hour period in the life of the main character, Jack Bauer. Jack would start off the day one way, and by the end of it, his entire reality had changed.

We're going to see the "original *24*" and see how God changed not just the reality of one man but the reality of an entire nation that was on the verge of disaster. Our story is in 2 Kings 7. There was a famine in the land, and it was so bad that people paid eighty pieces of silver for a donkey's head. They paid five pieces of silver for a little bit of dove's dung. Their entire economy was turned upside down, and it had gone on for so long that there was no end in sight. It was so bad that two mothers plotted to kill their own sons and eat them. The first one did, but when it came time for the second one to live up to her end of the bargain, she couldn't do it. She ran to the king to beg for his mercy.

What did the king do? He sent for the prophet Elisha, who made a bold prediction: "Hear ye the word of the LORD; Thus saith the LORD, To morrow about this time shall a measure of fine flour be sold for a shekel, and two measures of barley for a shekel, in the gate of Samaria" (v. 1). The prophet said that in twenty-four hours, God was going to take this nation from famine to feast and from depression to prosperity. Imagine prophesying that in the midst of an economic depression!

Here's how those in power responded to this prophetic word: "Then a lord on whose hand the king leaned answered the man of God, and said, Behold, if the LORD would make windows in heaven, might this thing be?" (v. 2). This man held a position of authority with the king—was one of his closest advisors—yet he responded with doubt instead of faith.

Elisha replied to the man, "Behold, thou shalt see it with thine eyes, but shalt not eat thereof" (v. 2). I don't want to be like this man, do you? Don't be the type of person who asks, "Can He?" That person will witness everyone else receiving the blessings that God has promised them while they miss out on all of it. And that's exactly what happened:

> And there were four leprous men at the entering in of the gate: and they said one to another, Why sit we here until we die? If we say, We will enter into the city, then the famine is in the city, and we shall die there: and if we sit still here, we die also. Now therefore come, and let us fall unto the host of the Syrians: if they save us alive, we shall live; and if they kill us, we shall but die. And they rose up in the twilight, to go unto the camp of the Syrians: and when they were come to the uttermost part of the camp of Syria, behold, there was no man there. For the LORD had made the host of the Syrians to hear a noise of chariots, and a noise of horses, even the noise of a great host.
>
> —vv. 3–6

Do you see what God did? A large army gathered around Israel to attack during the famine—yet God caused them to hear a noise of chariots, horses, and a great host. Those were some serious sound effects—the ultimate surround sound. The soldiers concluded that the king of Israel hired armies from numerous nations to come against them. They were so afraid that they fled for their lives without taking anything with them (v. 7). So when the lepers arrived in the camp, they found a bounty of food, supplies, weapons, clothes, and other provisions waiting for them to take.

God did exactly what He said He would. Within twenty-four hours, everything Elisha had prophesied came to pass. God completely turned the nation around financially—and I'm sure nobody thought He would use four lepers and some sound effects to pull it off.

And by the way, remember the king's advisor who doubted the word of Elisha? "The people trode upon him in the gate, and he died" (v. 20). Don't be like that faithless advisor. You don't need to worry about how God is going to do it. He has unlimited ways of doing things. He can do things that you can't even imagine. Instead of asking, "Can He do it?" declare boldly in faith, "Yes, He can!"

There are other examples throughout Scripture of individuals who doubted God. Psalm 78 talks about the children of Israel who doubted God: "Yea, they spake against God; they said, Can God furnish a table in the wilderness?" (v. 19). In the midst of battle, when God promised to protect and provide for them, "They turned back and tempted God, and limited the Holy One of Israel" (v. 41). Do you see that? They *limited God.* There is nothing on this earth that can stop God from doing what He promised you—except you. These individuals actually limited Him from being able to do all that He promised. They never made it into the Promised Land, and it wasn't because of God; it was because of their unbelief. They asked, "Can He?" instead of saying, "Yes, He can!"

People who grew up with Jesus doubted Him and were offended at Him—and the Bible says He could not do any mighty works among them.

People who grew up with Jesus doubted Him and were offended at Him—and the Bible says He could not do any mighty works among them (Mark 6). I don't doubt that He wanted to do those works, based on the Word of God and His actions, but He could not because of their unbelief. In fact, the Bible says He marveled at their unbelief. They were the kind of people who looked at Jesus and asked, "Can He?"

A few chapters later, in Mark 9, we meet a man who needed a devil cast out of his son. Yet the Word says Jesus did not immediately cast the devil out. Why? He couldn't—not while this man was saying, "*If* You can." He had to get the man to change his confession first. Jesus said, "No. If you can, believe. All things are possible to him that believeth." The man was limiting God, but once he understood, he said, "Lord, I believe. Help thou my unbelief"—and that is when Jesus cast the demon out of his son.

How about you? There are areas in your life where you need victory and God is ready to take you from famine to feast. Are you like the man who asked, "Can He?" If you are, the Enemy has been messing with you. He has been whispering in your ear and trying to convince you that God can't do what He said He was going to do. He whispers, *It's impossible. It's too late. It's too much.* You need to stop asking, "Can God do it? Can God work it out?" and instead say, "I know who I'm talking about. He's the almighty God. He's the King of kings and the Lord of lords. His arm is not short. Yes, He can!"

You need to proclaim Ephesians 3:20: "Now unto him that is able to do exceeding abundantly above all that we ask or think, according to the power that worketh in us." Why is this scripture in the Bible if God didn't want to do it? Yes, He can! I don't know what you are believing God for, but God can pull it off. He's got so many ways to pull it off that there's no way you can figure out how He's going to do it. If He turned around an entire nation using four lepers, He has a lot of ways to bring you from famine to feast. You just need to declare, "I know You can do it, God. I believe You, God. I trust You, God. I'm thanking You for it in advance."

Can God save your family? Can He heal your body? Can He give you a promotion? Can He prosper your business? Can He get you out of debt? Can He save your marriage? Yes, He can! He is the one who is able to do what needs to be done. Can He prosper your children? Can He save your loved ones and neighbors and co-workers? Can He turn a nation to Him? Whatever you need Him to do, He can do it!

I encourage you to meditate on these miracles that God has performed. They will remind you of His ability and that He can do anything for you no matter what you face:

- He created the world by His words.
- He defeated four armies with 318 servants.

- He blessed a 100-year-old man and his ninety-year-old barren wife with a child.
- He gave them six more kids after the husband turned 140.
- He made the barren fruitful, such as Hannah, Rebekah, Rachel, and Elizabeth.
- He made Isaac rich in a time of famine.
- He restored Jacob's wages and wealth.
- He gave Job twice what he lost.
- He made a thirty-year-old foreign slave and prisoner become prime minister overnight.
- He made the wicked of Egypt give their riches to the just Israel.
- He healed 2–3 million people through one meal.
- He parted the Red Sea.
- He gave manna from heaven.
- He gave millions of gallons of water from a rock.
- He made a Jewish woman the queen of Babylon.
- He stopped the sun in battle.
- He knocked down the walls of Jericho.
- He helped a seventeen-year-old boy defeat a giant in battle.
- He helped Samson kill a lion with his bare hands.
- He helped Samson defeat one thousand men with the jawbone of a donkey.
- He sent ravens to feed a man bread and meat.
- He multiplied oil—twice.
- He had fire fall from heaven to make a point.
- He made poison food edible.
- He made an iron float.
- He raised a man from the dead using another dead man's bones.
- He made a donkey talk.
- He defeated three armies without lifting a sword and left three days' harvest.

- He protected three men in a fiery furnace.
- He protected one man all night long from hungry lions.
- He had a fish swallow a man and spit him out alive and well.
- He spoke to a storm and the sea, and they obeyed.
- He walked on water.
- He multiplied five loaves and two fishes to feed five thousand.
- He multiplied seven loaves and two fishes to feed four thousand.
- He had a fish gobble up tax money and then delivered it to the man who needed it.
- He broke men out of prison—twice.
- He made the deaf hear.
- He made the blind see.
- He made the lame walk.
- He cleansed lepers.
- He raised the dead.
- He raised Himself from the dead.
- He saved all of mankind through one death.
- He made you righteous.
- He made heaven your home.

Tell the Devil to shut up, because you know the truth. You know that it may look bad. You may not be able to figure it out, and everybody else may think you're crazy, but God is on your side. And if God be for you, who can be against you? He can do what needs to be done. He can do more than what needs to be done. If He can turn a nation around in twenty-four hours, He can turn your situation around, too. Yes, He can! Nothing is impossible with God! Now, do your victory dance!

Turning Point

When the LORD turned again the captivity of Zion, we were like them that dream.

—PSALM 126:1

THIS FOURTH AND FINAL step in our challenge is entitled "Do Your Victory Dance," but you may still feel like you are far from dancing. You may be in a fight for your health, your marriage, your children, your finances, your ministry, your calling, or even your sanity. Whatever battle you are facing, ultimately you are in a fight with the Devil.

And there is something important about every great battle. There is always a turning point. If you look at history, you will see that. In World War II, there were two important turning points. One was D-Day, when the tide changed and Hitler started going backward in Europe instead of moving forward. The other is the Battle of Midway, the day when the United States started having success in the Pacific Front. More recently in our country, we had the Iraq surge. Whether you were for or against that war, everyone agreed that the surge was the turning point; when the military inserted more troops into Iraq, the situation turned, and suddenly we had an entirely different story happening in that country.

We see turning points throughout the Bible when God stepped into a situation and everything changed. The battle looked lost, but once God showed up, the battle was won for God and His people. Our key verse for today, Psalm 126, talks about how the Lord turned the captivity of Zion; they were in captivity, but He turned it around so that it almost seemed like a dream. They went from captivity to laughing and singing. In 2 Chronicles 20, all looked hopeless, and God said, "Stand and see the salvation of the Lord." All of a sudden, the enemy warriors turned on each other and Israel experienced victory. Later in the New Testament, the early church suffered great persecution, but when a man by the name of Saul converted, it was a turning point. The church was able to grow with much more freedom.

You may have a fight on your hands, but God is ready to step in and give you your turning point. Today, we're going to study what it takes to usher that turning point into our lives.

I looked up the definition of the phrase *turning point*. It's the point at which a very significant change occurs—a decisive moment, the point at which there is a change in direction or motion, a time or incident that marks the beginning of a completely new and usually better stage in somebody's life. I'll take that definition right there. Another definition says it's a

God never promised an easy ride—but He did promise a glorious victory.

landmark, an event marking a unique or historical change of course or one in which important developments depend.

When you get in a fight, you might wish it was over in thirty minutes, or even thirty days, but sometimes it takes much, much longer. God never promised an easy ride—but He did promise a glorious victory. He didn't say there won't be times when you may deal with some heavy situations, but that is not the end of the story: "Weeping may endure for a night but joy cometh in the morning.... Thou hast turned for me my mourning into dancing" (Psalm 30:5, 11). The psalmist is saying, "Lord, the situation was so bad, and I was mourning, but You got involved. When You stepped in and turned it around, I went from mourning to dancing."

Jesus said of Himself, quoting Isaiah 61, "The Spirit of the Lord is upon me, because he hath anointed me to preach the gospel...to give beauty for ashes, the oil of joy for mourning, the garment of praise of heaviness"

(Luke 4:18–19). You serve a God who will take your ashes and make beauty out of them—who will rebuild what was torn down.

Oftentimes, just when it seems darkest, your breakthrough is just around the corner. This is because Satan knows he has one last chance to beat you. If he doesn't win this battle, you've won. So he ratchets up the pressure on you for his one last opportunity to get you to quit. David's worst battle was at Ziklag, and when the enemy couldn't take him out, he became king. Joseph's darkest moment was when he was imprisoned—just before Pharaoh put a ring on his finger, making him prime minister of the kingdom.

You may be at that place where Pharaoh is about to put the ring on your finger, and you don't even know it because all seems lost. Someone is about to put that crown on your head. You are about to enter into that place of your calling that God has been talking to you about your entire life, and that is why you are under such a heavy attack. The Enemy understands that if you get through it, it is over for him. The damage is going to be great to his kingdom. God is going to be glorified. That is why the Enemy is trying to take you out.

So this isn't the time to concede defeat and say, "There is no future." This is the time to keep doing things God's way and believing that your turning point will come at any moment now. It is time to believe that breakthrough is imminent. When your turning point comes, not only will God turn it around for you, but He will enable you to take back for Him what—and who—belongs to Him.

"Hear, O our God; for we are despised: and turn their reproach upon their own head, and give them for a prey in the land of captivity" (Nehemiah 4:4). No wonder the Enemy is trying so hard to defeat you—he knows that someday you will find someone he still has a grip on, someone who is going to find themselves in hell one day, and you will tell this person the truth about Jesus. You will share your testimony that the Devil was dumb enough to give you. He was dumb enough to attack you, and you will be able to testify that God turned it around for you.

A Promise

God promises you a turnaround. "Seeing it is a righteous thing with God to recompense tribulation to them that trouble you" (2 Thessalonians 1:6). "The Lord shall cause thine enemies that rise up against thee to be smitten before thy face: they shall come out against thee one way, and flee before thee seven ways" (Deuteronomy 28:7).

Here are four things you need to do to help usher in your turning point.

1. Return to the Lord. "And shalt return unto the Lord thy God, and shalt obey his voice according to all that I command thee this day, thou and thy children, with all thine heart, and with all thy soul; that then the Lord thy God will turn thy captivity, and have compassion upon thee." (Deuteronomy 30:2–3). You see the pattern? You return to God, and you'll have those results. Read Job 22:23 and Joel 2:12, and you'll see the same principle.

2. Embrace the power of prayer. Make sure you are supplicating before God. Encourage other believers to pray with you about the situation, and God will turn it around.

3. Let God use you. "And the Lord turned the captivity of Job, when he prayed for his friends: also the Lord gave Job twice as much as he had before" (Job 42:10). Pray for others, even during your own time of need.

4. Stay the course. "Be ye therefore very courageous to keep and to do all that is written in the book of the law of Moses, that ye turn not aside therefrom to the right hand or to the left" (Joshua 23:6). What is it that you are not to turn from? Don't turn from your faith. Don't turn from your confession. Don't turn from your praise. Don't turn from living a lifestyle of holiness. Don't turn away from having faith in God. Have faith in God.

And when God does turn it around for you—and He will—be like the tenth leper who thanked Jesus and praised Him, not like the other nine who went on their way. Give God the praise and the glory and the honor that He is due. Then do your victory dance.

Day 28

Your Choice

"I have set before you life and death, blessing and cursing: therefore choose life, that both thou and thy seed may live."

—DEUTERONOMY 30:19

W**E'VE SPENT TWENTY-SEVEN DAYS** so far learning about victory. Now, on our final day together, I would like to offer you a choice. Actually, the Word of God is offering you a choice, because when the Word comes forth, you have a choice: You can accept it and have it in your life, or you can reject it and not experience it. Then you have your own self-fulfilling prophecy: "That message he preached, that Scripture he read—I didn't believe it." And then later on you can say, "Just as I thought, it didn't happen in my life." Of course it didn't happen—because you didn't believe it!

I will tell you something the Lord showed me not too long ago. The flesh wants to be unhappy. If you just go with the flesh, it doesn't matter what is going on; it will always find something to be unhappy about. Ninety-nine things could be right and one thing could be wrong, and the flesh wants you to dwell on the one thing that's wrong. So if you side with your flesh every day, it doesn't matter what is going on; you are going to be unhappy. Your spirit, on the other hand, always wants to be joyful. Your spirit is telling you, "Don't look at the ninety-nine things going wrong. Look at God and listen to what He's telling you."

A few days ago, we talked about turning points. Today—day twenty-eight—is a turning point for you. In every battle, there are moments where you feel like giving up. The intensity of the attack that the Devil launches against you is greater than you've ever had before. You may be at that point. God knows that once you break through this ceiling, that is it. You are going to have a huge impact for the kingdom of God, and there will be no looking back. Satan knows that, too. That's why he is trying so hard to stop you.

The question is, Do *you* know it? And the question is, What are you going to do about it? Will you discount the dozens of Scripture verses you've read in the past twenty-seven days? Will you throw away every promise of God that we've covered? Will you side with your flesh or with your spirit? Most importantly, will you side with what God says or what the Enemy says? It's your choice. I can't make it for you.

We are living in a time of substantial change, and all across the world you can see everything shifting to an entirely different level. It is time for you to rise up.

Today—day twenty-eight— is a turning point for you.

It is time for you to step fully into what God has planned for you. It is time for you to get from the back side of the desert where Moses was, get your staff, and face Pharaoh. It is time for you to be everything that God called you to be and do everything God has called you to do.

It's the time you have dreamed about. It's the time you have talked about. It's the time you have not even told other people about, because they wouldn't believe you. But you glimpsed it in the spirit. You can see what God is about to do. You don't understand it. You may not always have agreed with it. But now you are saying, "Oh, Lord. I can see it." You may be in the greatest fight of your life, but God is going to do what He said. He is going to work it out. He is going to turn it around. You are going to be right in the middle of it and say, "You are right, Lord, and it is wonderful in my eyes."

So you've got to a decision to make right now. I don't know what has happened in your past. Maybe you think the time is over for you. Maybe you believe the opportunity was there but you missed it. Maybe you are saying, "I failed, and my personal failure has sentenced me to a life of living beneath what God has put in my heart." Maybe other people have been telling you that you'll never experience victory in the areas you've been believing for.

Whatever it is, you must make a choice—a choice that you will not let that stop you from believing God. You can't allow that to keep you from dreaming the dream God has for you. This is your moment where you have to decide whether or not this story has a good ending. Your life is not destined to be a cautionary tale of what could have been. It will be that, though, if you decide to let whatever happened to you take you out. But the fact that you pressed through twenty-eight days and are still listening for what the Holy Spirit is saying to you today should be news to you that it is not too late.

It is never too late with God. You may have been delayed. You may have been derailed. But a delay is not permanent. Being derailed is not permanent. Whatever Satan did in your life is not permanent. It is temporary. It is only permanent if you let it be permanent. You may have felt God has been delayed. He has not. He never says no. He only says, "I have a better plan."

Will you choose to believe God's plan for your life—a plan for victory? Will you choose to apply what you've learned in the past twenty-eight days and pursue God like you never have before? It is your choice. I encourage you to pray this prayer:

> *Lord, I am not giving up. I choose to stick with this thing. I choose to continue to walk by faith. I choose to continue to live in integrity. I choose to continue to do it Your way.*
>
> *I fought this long. I prayed this long. I served You this long. I have confessed the Word this long. And I am not going to give up right at the end of this thing. I am busting through the door into the future You have for me.*
>
> *Lord, thank You for working it out, for turning it around, for giving me victory even in my midnight hours, for showing me*

again how good You are, how faithful You are, how awesome You are, how much You love me.

Thank You, Lord, that it is a done deal. You've done it again. You've made a river in the desert. You've made a way in the wilderness. You've parted my Red Sea. You've knocked down my Goliaths. You're healing my body, getting me out of debt, restoring my marriage, bringing home my kids, giving me favor on my job. Thank You for helping me get in Your perfect will for my life.

Thank You that the walls are falling right now, that You are moving right now, that You are confusing the Enemy right now. I am not hoping that it is done. I believe that it is done. And I thank You that it is already done. I am rejoicing because I know it is already done. I've already received it by faith, and I thank You for it.

Thank You for Your mercy when I've missed it—when I got in unbelief, when I stepped out of integrity and off Your path for me. You've given me second and third chances, and I'm so grateful You've gotten me to this point. You're turning it all around.

My life is for You. I live for You. I give You the honor and the glory that You are due. There is none like You. You are indescribable. You are uncontainable. You are the Most High God. You are so good, and I thank You for causing me to win in every area of my life.

Amen.

Now, do your victory dance!

I Can Win

1. What did you read during this section that surprised you or challenged you?

_____

_____

_____

_____

_____

_____

2. List "flashbacks" in your life that remind you of what God has done for you in the past.

_____

_____

_____

_____

_____

_____

_____

_____

3. As you read day twenty-seven, did the Holy Ghost bring to mind any long-forgotten dreams? What will you do about resurrecting them?

_____

_____

_____

_____

_____

_____

_____

_____

4. Quote two Scriptures, one from the Old Testament and one from the New Testament, that speak to you about that dream.

_____

_____

_____

_____

_____

_____

5. List the verses that God has quickened to you during this section. Use them as declarations during the next week to remind yourself of God's promises that you can win and be victorious, no matter what you face.

_____

_____

_____

_____

_____

_____

_____

_____

_____

6. Update the victory pages you filled out on day one. In which areas have you seen victory?

_____

_____

_____

_____

_____

Recommended Resources

André Butler's other books and resources on how to live victoriously:

God's Future for You
Not in My House!
Living Life to the Full
Winning the War Within
The Missing Element
Getting to Your Promised Land
God Is Making You Rich
Gaining Financial Freedom
Wealth of the Sinner, Harvest of the Just
The One Another Principle
Seedtime and Harvest: Receiving the Fullness of Your Harvest
God's Plan for the Church
God's Plan for the Single Saint

About the Author

ANDRÉ BUTLER IS DEDICATED to helping individuals experience the future God has for them. He accomplishes this mission through serving as senior pastor of Word of Faith International Christian Center in Southfield, Michigan, and through speaking engagements, "Your Future Now" broadcasts and podcasts, Facebook, Twitter, YouTube, CDs, MP3s, books, and much more. We invite you to connect with André on Facebook, Twitter, and YouTube, as well as to be a guest at Word of Faith.

If You're a Fan of This Book, Please Tell Others...

- Write about *You Can Win* on your blog, Twitter, and Facebook page.
- Suggest *You Can Win* to friends.
- When you're in a bookstore, ask them if they carry the book. The book is available through all major distributors, so any bookstore that does not have *You Can Win* in stock, can easily order it.
- Write a positive review of *You Can Win* on www.amazon.com.
- Send my publisher, HigherLife Publishing, suggestions on websites, conferences, and events you know of where this book could be offered at media@ahigherlife.com.
- Purchase additional copies to give away as gifts.

Connect With Us...

To learn more about *You Can Win,* please contact us at:

Word of Faith
20000 W. Nine Mile Road
Southfield, MI 48075
www.wordoffaith.cc
(248) 353-3476 or (800) 541-PRAY (7729) (24-hour prayer)

Facebook: www.facebook.com/pages/Andre-Butler/190218697136
Twitter: @andrebutler
YouTube: www.youtube.com/pastorandrebutler

You may also contact my publisher directly:

HigherLife Publishing
400 Fontana Circle, Building 1 – Suite 105
Oviedo, Florida 32765
Phone: (407) 563-4806
Email: media@ahigherlife.com